T0295618

African Luxury Branding

Bringing together critical race, queer and decolonial analytical approaches, visual analysis, and multimodal discourse analysis, this book explores the discursive strategies deployed by African luxury brands in an age of cross-platform, intertextual branding.

Building on literature examining the aesthetics and politics of African luxury, this book demonstrates how leading African luxury brands create visual material speaking to complex sensibilities of culture, nature, and future. Iqani shows how powerful brand narratives and strategies reveal ethical and ideological messages that function to re-position Africa in an increasingly congested global marketplace of ideas. In acknowledging that there is a strong political validity to recognizing the importance of African brands staking their claim in luxury, this book also problematizes the role these brands play in the promotion of luxury discourses, advancing the project of capitalism and their contribution to broader patterns of inequality.

Shedding new light not only on luxury branding strategies but also on the idea of a luxurious global "Africanicity" and on the complex cultural politics of South Africa, African Luxury Branding will be of interest to advanced students and researchers in disciplines, including Critical Advertising Studies, African Studies, Media and Communications.

Mehita Iqani is the South African Research Chair in Science Communication at Stellenbosch University, South Africa.

Routledge Critical Advertising Studies
Series Editor: Jonathan Hardy

Routledge Critical Advertising Studies tracks the profound changes that have taken place in the field of advertising. Presenting thought-provoking scholarship from both prominent scholars and emerging researchers, these ground-breaking short form publications cover cutting-edge research concerns and contemporary issues within the field. Titles in the series explore emerging trends, present detailed case studies and offer new assessments of topics such as branded content, economic surveillance, product placement, gender in marketing, and promotional screen media. Responding quickly to the latest developments in the field, the series is intellectually compelling, refreshingly open, provocative, and action-oriented.

Branded Entertainment and Cinema
The Marketisation of Italian Film
Gloria Dagnino

Branding Diversity
New Advertising and Cultural Strategies
Susie Khamis

Branded Entertainment in Korea
Hyunsun Yoon

African Luxury Branding
From Soft Power to Queer Futures
Mehita Iqani

Consumer Society and Ecological Crisis
Leslie M. Meier

For more information about this series, please visit: https://www.routledge.com/Routledge-Critical-Advertising-Studies/book-series/RCAS

African Luxury Branding

From Soft Power to Queer Futures

Mehita Iqani

Routledge
Taylor & Francis Group

LONDON AND NEW YORK

First published 2023
by Routledge
4 Park Square, Milton Park, Abingdon, Oxon OX14 4RN

and by Routledge
605 Third Avenue, New York, NY 10158

*Routledge is an imprint of the Taylor & Francis Group, an
informa business*

© 2023 Mehita Iqani

British Library Cataloguing-in-Publication Data
A catalogue record for this book is available from the British
Library

Library of Congress Cataloguing-in-Publication Data
Names: Iqani, Mehita, author.
Title: African luxury branding : from soft power to queer
futures / Mehita Iqani.
Description: Abingdon, Oxon ; New York, NY : Routledge, 2023. |
Series: Routledge critical advertising studies | Includes
bibliographical references and index. |
Identifiers: LCCN 2022031173 | ISBN 9781032129617
(hardback) | ISBN 9781032129624 (paperback) | ISBN
9781003227038 (ebook)
Subjects: LCSH: Branding (Marketing)--Africa. | Luxuries--
Africa. |
Selling--Luxuries--Africa. | Luxuries--Social aspects--Africa.
Classification: LCC HF5415.1255 .I39 2023 | DDC
658.827096--dc23/eng/20220629
LC record available at https://lccn.loc.gov/2022031173

ISBN: 978-1-032-12961-7 (hbk)
ISBN: 978-1-032-12962-4 (pbk)
ISBN: 978-1-003-22703-8 (ebk)

DOI: 10.4324/9781003227038

Typeset in Times New Roman
by MPS Limited, Dehradun

Contents

Figures

Acknowledgements

Every effort has been made to trace and contact copyright holders, but this has not been possible in every case. The publishers would be pleased to hear from any copyright holders not acknowledged here so that this section may be amended at the earliest opportunity.
This book has been a long time in the planning and writing, as I have been thinking critically about luxury for several years.

In the first instance, I am grateful to the creative minds who have produced the artworks, luxury objects, and imagery that got me thinking, and who have given me permission to reproduce some of their work in this book. To all the research participants that I cite in this book, as well as those that I didn't cite here: thank you for sharing your insight and expertise about the African luxury industry and helping me to shape my thinking on this topic.

Thank you to the Governing Intimacies project, especially Professor Srila Roy, for funding support that helped me buy some free time to complete this writing. This research was also supported by an African Humanities Programme grant and writing residency at Makerere University, a South African National Research Foundation grant, and a fantastic writing residency at the Stellenbosch Institute for Advanced Study, which I'll never forget and hope I get to do again some day.

My thanks also to everyone who listened to my ideas, suggested case studies, put me in touch with people to approach for interviews, or told me about luxury spaces I should visit, or in other ways supported this project: David du Preez, Brett Rogers, Nat Iqani, Nicky Falkof, Gina Waldman, Cobus van Staden, Lebogang Mogashoa, Katlego Disemelo, Maya Loon, Hayley Gewer, Bettina Malcomess.

I am grateful to the research assistants who helped with interview transcription and literature reviewing, particularly Tessa Hellberg but also Hlonepho Phakoe, Jessie Schultz, and Vicky Amupulo. Appreciation to Gabriel Shamu who helped me source image permissions.

My thanks to the team at Routledge, and the Critical Advertising Studies series editor, Jonathan Hardy, for seeing the potential in my book proposal, and to the reviewers for their helpful feedback.

In some ways this book is my small ode to Johannesburg, a city in which I lived for a decade, and which consistently challenged and inspired me. Although complex and unfair, Johannesburg is also a city that never ceases to inspire. Johannesburg's love of creativity and luxury and the brilliant people that it attracts with its promises of fame, fortune, and fun, who go there to live and fulfil their dreams, are its biggest assets despite its lovely, rolling, rocky koppies, lush green suburbs, and twinkling cityscapes. As a highly unequal city, Jozi has its share of misery and luxury both. My study of the luxury that is celebrated in Johannesburg, and other African cities like it, is intended to contributed to bigger debates about inequality, what it looks and feels like, and how it might be overcome, in this city, country, and continent. We need to see both wealth and poverty to understand how to transcend both.

1 African Luxury Brands in Global and Local Context

In the past decade, Africa has been reviving in the global popular imagination. The huge success of the blockbuster film *Black Panther (2018)*, and the wide visibility of Black Lives Matter protests have contributed to Africa, associated as it is with global Black cultures, escaping from the homogenizing, minimizing, and negative stereotypes that were historically forced on it by the West. Multiple positive narratives of Africa and Africanness are being actively constructed in media culture every day by a wide variety of intellectual, cultural, and creative movements. One key player in this reinstatement of African cultures to their rightful place alongside others in the world's marketplace of ideas, as this book will show, is the emergence of luxury brands from within the continent. From all corners of this richly diverse continent on which I am privileged to live, learn, and research, creative entrepreneurs have designed and produced bold, beautiful, and highly desirable consumer brands and commodities that have been intentionally situated within the luxury industry. These African luxury brands have been received, indeed coveted, with great enthusiasm by a diverse range of consumers in African countries, the African diaspora, and beyond. Global superstars like Beyoncé proudly feature the clothing of African designers on their bodies and in their music videos, and African designers are increasingly entering into collaborations with long-established global luxury brands or being featured on the platforms of highly prestigious international fashion platforms.

This short book explores some of the key sensibilities and modalities of branding by African luxury labels and companies. My aim is both to show how powerful such communications can be, in the context of a diversifying global culture industry, and also to critically reflect on the ways in which African luxury branding furthers the project of capitalism in complex ways that are at once empowering and contribute to broader patterns of inequality. The focus of this book will be to

DOI: 10.4324/9781003227038-1

critically explore the discursive strategies deployed by African luxury brands: it will examine the brand messaging and iconic aesthetic forms of selected African luxury brands, which are once part of a wave of Afro-optimism, itself a complex debate (Bond, 2014; Havnevik, 2015; Onwudiwe and Ibelema, 2003), and key players contributing to a rewriting of the place of African businesses in the global economy. There is a strong political validity to recognizing the importance of African brands staking their claim in luxury, and an optimistic, idealistic even, sensibility will be evident in this book. However, I will also problematize the role these brands play in the promotion of wealth as the destination for the improvement of life in settings of gross inequality produced by legacies of injustice.

From a business perspectives, Africa and Africans are certainly considered to be a promising current and future market for global branding and distribution of a wide variety of commodities, luxury versions included (Iqani, 2019; Mahajan, 2011). Although Africa has not typically been associated with luxury by white and Western observers, the appetite for it among Africans is sincere, though Africa still represents only a small part of the global market share. Outside of the West, luxury consumer markets are dominated by the Middle East (Moser and Narayanamurthy, 2016; Ramadan and Nsouli, 2021) and East Asia, especially China (Chevalier and Lu, 2011; Cui et al., 2015), with growing spending in Latin America (Diniz, 2014) and South Asia (Atwal and Jain, 2012; Kuldova, 2016). Building on existing work exploring the aesthetics and politics of African luxury (Iqani and Dosekun, 2019), this book explores the messaging and aesthetics of purposively selected, leading-edge, contemporary African luxury brands.

The stereotyping of Africa and Africans is an ongoing problem that scholars should continue to study and critique (Bunce et al., 2016). In this book, I work to put aside, temporarily, these long-standing (and at times rather tiresome) debates about the extent to which Africa and Africans are consistently mis-represented and stereotyped in global media discourses. Instead, my aim is to focus on the luxury brand aesthetics emerging from the continent, both to show that they exist, but also to explore how they are producing innovative aesthetics and narratives that reach global cultural markets. As such, the very existence of African luxury brands counters discourses about the long-stereotyped "dark continent." Integrating analyses of interviews with luxury brand makers working in Africa with critical visual analysis of the products of their labours – the brand imagery shared publicly on promotional communications platforms – this book shows the power and promise of African luxury branding in the 21st century.

It also reveals the aesthetic and discursive complexity attendant to branding luxury in the age of "Africa rising" (Taylor, 2014), and the corresponding increase in inequality that characterizes much of social life and politics in the global south. For, although the existence of African luxury speaks to an important political project about the equality of all cultural production, so too does it highlight the persistent and growing power of capitalism and global commercial discourses.

Critical Perspectives on African Luxury

In order to contextualize the original empirical and theoretical claims made in this study, it is necessary to synthesize the key themes that illuminate existing critical research addressing luxury in general, and in Africa specifically.

The Spirit of Luxury: Administrative and Critical Approaches

A well-established and growing body of literature exists that takes luxury as its focus. A significant amount of early work on luxury was situated within brand management and marketing studies, and tended to focus on either analysing the operations of the luxury market or on providing empirically rooted advice on how better to market luxury goods to consumers. This genre of research can be summarized as managerialist and administrative (Lazarsfeld, 1941) in nature, and firmly located within the pragmatics of business studies. Some work has mapped out the characteristics of luxury brands (Vigneron and Johnson, 2004) in general, or the specific personality traits of luxury fashion brands (Heine, 2010; Okonkwo, 2016). Other work has focused on the managerial aspects of luxury business, for example, in work on the core communication strategies of fashion brands (Jin and Cedrola, 2017), or on the business of luxury branding in general; or on what can be learned from specific case studies like luxury goods company LVMH and its brand management strategies (Cavender and Kincade, 2014). The definitive handbook in the business of luxury management is *Luxury Brand Management* (Chevalier and Mazzalovo, 2012), which sets out in exhaustive detail the definitions and markers of luxury brands, the major luxury sectors (ready-to-wear fashion, perfumes, wines and spirits, watches and jewellery, and leather goods), as well as industry know-how from branding to communications to customer management, retail, and licensing. Other work has looked at how luxury brands are perceived in relation to status and conspicuousness (Truong et al., 2008). In the niche of brand management research, there are several studies that consider consumer perceptions on luxury, for example, what consumers see as the characteristics of luxury goods (Walley et al., 2013), how individualism and collectivism influence purchase decision-making (Aliyev and Wagner, 2018), on how externalized (status-oriented) versus internalized (style-oriented) forms luxury consumption should inform luxury retail management (Amatulli and Guido, 2012), how brand communities are a key site through which loyalty to particular luxury car brands is developed (Loureiro and Kaufmann, 2016), and how luxury brands can sell their wares online (Larraufie and Kourdoughli, 2014; Okonkwo, 2010; Seringhaus, 2005). One study explored the links between materialism, luxury consumption, and happiness in Dutch-speaking Belgium (Hudders and Pandelaere, 2011) and found that among more "materialistic" consumers luxury consumption did make them happier. This management-oriented literature is united by an orientation towards branding as professional practice, and exhibits a normative view of business practice as central to economic development. It therefore orients its contributions to understanding luxury towards the administration of its business interests.

In contrast, an alternative set of views located in the critical humanities tradition explores luxury from cultural, social, and political perspectives. Although the idea of luxury has existed and been theorized in western thought since antiquity, it was perhaps first conceptualized in the contemporary terrain of critical humanities scholarship by Christopher Berry (Berry, 1994), who both put luxury into historical context and provided a critical vocabulary for explaining how luxury is defined and deployed commercially and culturally. About twenty years later, in the US context, James Twitchell argued that the rise of luxury consumption was indicative of a mainstreaming of high end materialism and promotional culture (Twitchell, 2013). These studies frame luxury as sociologically and culturally situated within questions of aesthetics, class identity, and the political economy of late capitalism, and show the evolution of thinking about luxury and how the term has come to be central to consumer aesthetics in contemporary culture. In the 20 or so years, since luxury came into the vocabulary of critical cultural theorists, a range of work has been published that explores some or other aspect of it. Patrizia Calefato explores the aesthetic and cultural resonances of luxury, arguing that it "is waste, exceptional possession, distinction without a price" and "also the ineluctable ascent toward the spaces of desire, where magnificence and splendour are exalted" (Calefato, 2014: 7). In their 2016 book, Peter McNeil and Giorgio Riello tell the history of luxury from an object-centred perspective, arguing that luxury is not an immutable category (McNeil and

Riello, 2016) and should be understood to be relative and context dependent. Luxury can be defined as an elite area of consumer culture, in which high-end goods are manufactured and sold at great expense to consumers with access to spending power. As such, narratives of exclusivity, leisure, artistry, quality, rarity, and value are associated with luxury. Mike Featherstone has written both about luxury as a sumptuary system (Featherstone, 2014), and theorized luxury in relation to the ancient Roman notion of "luxus," or debauchery and excess (Featherstone, 2016). As is evident so far, the notion of luxury provokes a number of historical, aesthetic, sociological, and poetic ruminations from scholars based in and thinking from the West.

The field of critical luxury studies is the most salient theoretical foundation for this book. As John Armitage and Joanne Roberts explicate (Armitage and Roberts, 2016a), in western thought luxury has a long provenance, having been moralized, de-moralized, and re-moralized since the 18th century. Summarizing this evolution as the "spirit of luxury" Armitage and Roberts (2016b) argue that luxury is a pre-eminent site through which critical research on capitalism can and must take place. Critical luxury studies, they argue, is a new academic field that draws on historical understandings of luxury and engages with the complex social, cultural, political, economic, and indeed environmental implications of luxury objects, subjects, and practices (Armitage and Roberts, 2016a: 1–2). In contrast to a management studies approach, that does not concern itself "with the ethics of the growing inequality upon which their business models depend," a critical approach seeks to directly engage with difficult questions about power, empowerment, and the "increasing concentration of wealth" (Armitage and Roberts, 2016a: 7) introduced by luxury. This book situates itself within the critical approach to luxury, but also recognizes that the brand management domain exerts considerable influence over the realities of luxury consumption and discourse in the world. Critical scholarship needs to pay as much attention to the practices, ideologies, and ideals of those working within the luxury industry as it does to the images, brands, commodities, and cultures that are produced by it.

One of the key theoretical foundations for research to do with luxury and the wealthy is the theory of conspicuous consumption (Veblen, 2007), in which it was argued that it was through an orientation to material goods that the working classes of Europe achieved social mobility and the "leisure class" distinguished itself from others. "For Veblen, the concept of conspicuous consumption denotes the acquisition of luxury goods and services in order to publicly display one's economic power, either through one's income or through one's accumulated wealth" (Armitage and Roberts, 2016a: 5–6). Thus, Veblen saw luxury as a "facet of consumerism" and "social stratification," which was based on the "division of labour," and as such an inherently useless activity that did not contribute in any meaningful way to the functioning of society (Armitage and Roberts, 2016a: 6). In a similar vein, three quarters of a century later, the theory of "distinction" (Bourdieu, 1984) outlined how consumption functions as a form of social positioning, and that by undertaking forms of consumption associated with the upper classes, lower classes could climb the social ladder or at least be perceived to be doing so. This perspective on luxury has had a significant influence on critical scholarship on consumption in general, which can tend towards implying that any form of pleasurable consumption should be considered morally and socially bankrupt. Without abandoning the importance of bringing a critique to the social stratifications that produce wealth and narrate consumption as the only path to happiness and success, it is nevertheless overly simplifying to only see luxurious consumption from this extremely critical perspective. Without a doubt, pleasure and leisure are more complex social activities than the simple display of status. Sometimes, consumption is framed as luxurious by virtue of saving the consumer time, for example through paying extra for a priority queue (Nickel, 2016). Further, consumption has been understood by anthropologists and scholars of material culture, to be a key modality through which human relations are forged and maintained (Miller, 1997, 1998, 2001, 2013).

Another key avenue through which work on luxury has taken place is on the subject of the super-rich. Some important work has been done about the extremes of inequality in the global economy (Haseler, 2000; Hay and Beaverstock, 2016; Jaworski and Thurlow, 2017; Roberts, 2019; Serafini and Maguire, 2019). Key debates in this sub-set of literature on luxury raise questions about the moral claims (and immorality) of such extremes of income, the political-economic structures that have created and maintained elite wealth, and the consumption practices of the super-rich themselves. Significant attention has also been paid to the geographies of super-wealth (Atkinson, 2016; Beaverstock et al., 2004; Forrest et al., 2017; Hay, 2013; Hay and Muller, 2012), mapping out the ways in which extreme wealth has impacted on cities in particular, but also on to cultures of travel and consumption. This ties in with growing work on social inequality (Dorling, 2015; Francis et al., 2020; Irvin, 2008), that puts the question of extreme wealth into direct relation with the problems of extreme poverty. From this perspective, luxury consumption is the material manifestation of highly unjust forms of social inequality, produced through centuries of capitalist exploitation and the economic oppression of the working classes, people of colour and women. Luxury and poverty are both the products of capitalism. For those who have the wealth to buy yachts, sportscars, luxury homes, and so on, as they wish, not to mention amass huge collections of outrageously expensive fashion items, watches, and personal services, luxury becomes a way of life that defines and justifies their elite status, while the rest of the world – the 99% – look on in envy or anger, while they struggle to pay school fees, feed their families, or provide for their own basic daily needs.

As this summary of key literature so far has shown, critical thinking on luxury has included arguments that suggest an affinity towards luxury is a form of jostling for social recognition and position, and arguments that centre the role of capital, either celebratorily or critically. Luxury is intimately linked with economic inequality as well as cultural capital, and in the post-modern world, it is increasingly necessary to understand luxury in relation to arts, design, and media, and the attendant political-economies that shape these cultural spheres (Armitage and Roberts, 2016b). Studying luxury is an important entry point into broader considerations of the shape and operations of global capitalism and its attendant inequalities. The positioning of luxury as a key point for exploring the problem of inequality is a useful interface with considering how luxury outside of the West has been theorized and researched.

Luxury is African: Contesting Western-centric Views

As Armitage and Roberts point out, "luxury defies objective definition" and "varies across time and space" (Armitage and Roberts, 2016a: 12). The concept of luxury, in Africa as well as elsewhere, is a conglomeration of ideas. It includes the surface notion of shine (Cheng, 2011b; Thompson, 2015) – glossy desirability, social aspiration and product perfection somehow all rolled into one – and deeper level ideas about craftsmanship, cultural heritage, and rarity – a manifold rationale for higher price points combined. Luxury "is a place of struggle of various forms of indulgence" (Armitage and Roberts, 2016a: 14). One of the key fissure points in the struggle to define, own, and promote luxury has to do with the global geo-politics of consumption.

Early on in my research into African luxury (which I discuss methodologically later in this chapter, and in the appendix), I made the mistake of sometimes explicitly asking my interlocutors whether they think that luxury suffers from being overly defined as something emanating from the West. Although some of my participants used famous western luxury brands as reference points to explain what luxury means to them and in general, I found that they did not in any way see these values as antithetical to African material cultures and production values (Iqani, 2020, 2021). In one interview, I was speaking with the founder and designer of a luxury fashion brand based in a large West African city. Although I regret this framing now, I asked my interlocuter, whom I anonymize as Esmé, "Do you think we are still stuck in a space where we rely on western ideas of luxury?" and she responded, with some irritation in her voice, "I wouldn't say *western* idea of what luxury is, what is a *western* idea of luxury?" To Esmé, luxury is luxury, and to put the prefix western or African onto it is irrelevant. To her, quality is quality, the best is the best. From the perspective of material indicators, including excellent service and fine craftsmanship, there is something universal about how luxury is defined. As this important conversation shows, any assumption that luxury is inherently Western, or that Western branding and consumer culture are the primary paradigms through which luxury is defined, is problematic. Esmé taught me that it is necessary to delink the concept of luxury from the dominance of western capitalism.

Luxury is fuelled by the "logic of exclusion" (Rocamora, 2016: 216), in other words it never offers to be available to everyone. One of the inherent contradictions of the capitalist economy, particularly the postmodern and neoliberal form that dominates globally, is that it excludes in practice what it includes in discourse. In other words, while economic structures produce inequality, poverty, extreme wealth, and make every opportunity to participate in public or material life depend on having money, and actively excludes those who do not have riches or access to credit, the language of neoliberalism (advertising, branding, influencing) promises – falsely – that capitalism is linked to democracy, equality, fairness, and the possibility that everyone can access its comforts and pleasures. This contradiction plays out on a global scale, where the "haves" (broadly speaking, the industrialized wealthy countries) enjoy a better quality of life and access to material comforts than the "have-nots" (broadly speaking, countries struggling to rebuild after legacies of colonial ravaging). The global divide between having and not having has been described as a split between global north and south (Levander and Mignolo, 2011). This is a welcome move away from polarizing terms such as developed/developing or first/third worlds, but it should not be taken to be a geographic binary. The rich, middle class, or otherwise resourced population is threaded across every so-called "poor" country, and precarious, hungry, and resourceless people are likewise threaded into the fabric of every "rich" country. Taking the birds-eye view of the global economy and its haves and have-nots, which were produced by the matrix of colonialism, slavery, patriarchy, and all the other forms of exclusion that made a minority wealthy at the expense of the many, there is a historic reason for seeing luxury as the preserve of the wealthy west, while the rest are considered as the mass excluded because they cannot afford it. But, as I will show in this book, the notion that luxury comes from the West has only been constructed as "true" (largely by western scholarship on luxury) and must therefore be deconstructed. My argument is that an Anglo- or Euro-centric conception of luxury is not useful as theoretical framework for considering luxury in general, and certainly in relation to Africa.

Luxury has typically been framed as a West vs Rest topic, in the key foundational literature of the field. For example, in *Luxury, A Rich History*, consumers outside the global north are summarized as "the *new* global luxury consumer" (McNeil and Riello, 2016: 249–251 – emphasis added), and the discussion focuses on the assumption that Asian, Latin American, and African consumers deploy their growing spending power to buy western luxury brands. Luxury consumption sometimes comes up in studies about the so-called new middle classes emerging in post-colonial contexts, as well as in Western critiques of elites in those settings. The subtext to labelling consumption "new" is that luxury is framed as normal in western economies yet somehow unusual in other settings, and further that when luxury exists in the latter it is imported and therefore not a natural part of the host society or economy. I summarize this theoretical attitude as the *luxury mimesis* position: it presumes that luxury is endemic to the west and implies that when it exists elsewhere it is imitative. There is a growing managerialist literature that explores the growth of luxury consumption in non-western contexts and takes this mimetic position as the norm. China and India have received a significant amount of attention, mostly because of the huge populations in these countries and the growth of middle- and upper-income consumers as a result of their recent industrialization and economic growth. The history and contemporary shape of luxury business and markets in China has been summarized in detail (Chevalier and Lu, 2011; Rovai, 2016), and multiple perspectives on how Chinese consumers engage with luxury have been presented (Wang and Song, 2013). The mimetic position is linked with managerialist scholarship that aims to contribute to the deployment of marketing strategies and business insights (usually to the benefit of western capital). Such thinking is underscored by the assumption that development means that other parts of the world will, or should, start to act and look like western economies and that consumers there will "evolve" until they behave like western consumers. This reproduces some aspects of the cultural imperialism thesis, which sees the export of Western culture as a one-way conduit for domination (Schiller, 1976). The notion of cultural imperialism has been replaced with more complex theories of media globalization, seeing cultural flows as multi-directional, albeit not always equal in power (see Hardy, 2014).

In the context of non-western consumer cultures, luxury has often been framed – problematically I would argue – as "conspicuous consumption." Where consumption is theorized one-dimensionally as a route to social mobility and the performance of status, the acquisition and display of high-end, expensive, luxury products is also theorized, likewise one-dimensionally, as an attempt to demonstrate elite status. The idea of conspicuous consumption has been re-loaded in several ways, for example in work examining "bling" culture in hip-hop music videos (Hunter, 2011), and on the excessive consumption of global south politicians (Iqani, 2016). Research has examined the emergence of the luxury market in China (Cui et al., 2015; see also Zhiyan et al., 2013), and the current market for luxury goods in India into historical perspective (Atwal and Jain, 2012). More work is required that expands our understandings of luxury and de-westernizes existing theories of luxury consumption. This book contributes to this project.

The analysis of African luxury brands should also be situated within African Studies approaches to consumer culture. Much has been written about fashion cultures in west Africa (Brodin et al., 2016; Newell, 2012), as well as the role of "dandy" fashion on historical diamond mines in South Africa (Magubane, 2004). Studies of consumer culture in South Africa have focused on historical accounts of the links between colonialism and consumption (Burke, 1996), apartheid and consumption (Posel, 2010) and on the rise of new middle classes and their practices of aspiration, expenditure, and consumption (Iqani, 2015; James, 2014; Laden, 2003).

Patrizia Calefato, in a very brief discussion of a 2000 Diesel advertising campaign that showed wealthy Africans enjoying themselves, comments that its

> shock effect was based on the fact that Western readers are well aware that in African cities, as in the rest of the postcolonial world, the wealthy live in the greatest luxury, while the majority live in conditions of utmost poverty.
>
> (Calefato, 2014: 66)

It is precisely this stereotype – that Africa is the site of poverty and any wealth that exists is exceptional and always exploiting regimes of poverty – that is perpetuated through a great deal of existing research on luxury. Africa is mentioned in western luxury scholarship often on these terms, as though luxury is a foreign concept, imported from elsewhere, "shockingly" enjoyed by the wealthy at the expense of most others living in miserable "utmost poverty." The luxury mimesis position takes specific shape in the context of African material. Inequality exists in Africa as does poverty, but the perpetuation of stereotype through luxury scholarship eclipses alternative narratives about what wealth and luxury mean, in general and in Africa in specific. This book aims to expand and diversify the scholarly conversation dramatically, building on the assertion made by myself and Simidele Dosekun (Iqani and Dosekun, 2019: 5):

> African luxury as we call it heuristically, is equal in aesthetic, if not economic and cultural, stature to other formations of luxury, and it plays a constitutive role in the contemporary global luxury economy and its politics.

Little scholarly research has focused on luxury consumption in Africa, though some important new work is changing this. The book co-edited by myself, titled *African Luxury: Aesthetics and Politics* (Iqani and Dosekun, 2019) presents a cross-section of interdisciplinary scholarship looking at different aspects of luxury on the continent, including notably a chapter by Mokoena (2019) critically discussing from an Africanist perspective the Diesel advertising campaign mentioned above. My work on African celebrity selfies and "new" yuppies (Iqani, 2016) touches on questions of luxury, and links with studies of "hyperfeminine" fashion subjectivities in Lagos, Nigeria (Dosekun, 2020), yuppie sensibilities in Nairobi, Kenya (Spronk, 2012), and good time girls and socialites (Ligaga, 2014, 2016) also in Kenya. It is notable that this work emerges from an African feminist epistemology, and a nuanced understanding of gender politics and its intersection with consumer cultures. As the rest of this book will show, questions of how gender is performed in African luxury brands often intersect with aspirational discourses across the urbanized sectors of the continent.

Researching African Luxury Branding: Notes on Methods

This book is situated within Critical Luxury Studies in that does not simply seek to criticize luxury, but "adopts a view *within* the object of study" in order to elucidate both what enables and constrains it as a discourse (Armitage and Roberts, 2016b: 12). The evidence and arguments presented in this book were gleaned through a decolonial discourse analysis of purposively selected case studies, contextualized and put into dialogue, where useful, with material from ethnographic work.

Decolonial Visual Analysis of Black-owned South African Luxury Brands

The book chooses to take a specific focus on Black-owned South African luxury brands. This specific empirical framing was chosen for practical and conceptual reasons. Practically, being South African gives me the benefit of proximity and a contextual understanding of the market and culture in the country. There are other, more important, reasons for the chosen focus. South Africa is one of the strongest economies on the continent (David and Grobler, 2020), and as such produces significant economic activity, and is a member of the BRICS formation of major emerging economies globally (Thussu and Nordenstreng, 2015). Although there are many important luxury brands emanating from other African countries, and there are important links and connections between South African brands and other African brands, mapping those is a project which cannot be achieved in the limits of this short book. I recommend this project to future research and other writers. The brands chosen as case studies for discussion in this book are based in South Africa, Black-owned and celebrate pan-African and "Afropolitan" (Farber, 2010; Fasselt, 2015) aesthetics and values, even though they are rooted in and emerge from the South African creative economy. Because I myself am South African, and work in the South African higher education sector, these choices although natural were also strategic, as it allowed for a closer, more nuanced explication of some aspects of the milieu in which the brands operate. I choose to analyse the brand imagery presented in this book in the context of "Africanness" rather than "South Africanness" as this is the strongest key messaging that seems to emerge from the material. As the book will show, luxury brand communicators deploy the ideas of Africa and African in special ways, that transcend the nation and its politics and connect with globalized sensibilities of Black and African cultures. As such, they speak more to a luxurious global "Africanicity" (Dosekun, 2019) than the complex cultural politics of South Africa specifically.

   There are many white-owned luxury businesses operating on the continent, especially in South Africa (the economic legacy of Apartheid that economically privileged white people is the clear reason for this). Often white-owned brands intentionally use what they see as African aesthetics in order to market themselves. A case in point is the highly lucrative "safari" industry, which uses the aesthetic of an unpeopled landscape to sell a mythic connection to the land and wilderness to well-heeled international tourists and wealthy locals (Falkof, 2022; Musila, 2015; Nixon, 2013). This links to colonial histories in which conquering "explorers" framed the land as empty, wild and available for the taking (see Pratt, 2008). In South Africa, which has a significant and economically privileged minority (8%) white population, there seems to be an assumption that it is acceptable to use "Black" aesthetics to brand local businesses, as a way to suggest local authenticity and political legitimacy. This is a form of cultural appropriation (Lenard and Balint, 2020): non-Black-owned commercial entities using Black and African aesthetics to sell their wares. Although this is a very important area of possible research – how white owned businesses try to present their values and aesthetics as sympathetic to or emanating from Black cultures, which I encourage other researchers to take up, this is not the focus of the work I do in this book.

I choose to focus explicitly on African luxury brands that are Black-owned, and in which the owner of the brand (the person that often is the brand themselves), is a Black African and public figure who shows themselves as such as part of their marketing. It follows that some of the case studies chosen for analysis in this book (which will be discussed in detail in the chapters that follow) are individuals who have achieved fame and success through branding their identities, closely linked to their creative and cultural production of value in the aesthetic economy. Their personal brands are considered to be part of the luxury industry in that even when they do not necessarily sell luxury goods, they embody an affiliation to and sensibility of luxury (quality, rarity, elegance, avant-garde aesthetics). Some of the brands analysed are medium enterprizes with global aspirations, others are smaller, personal brands that sometimes collaborate with established global brands. It would not be an overstatement to suggest that all aspire for global recognition and market access; some have already achieved it. An expansive definition of luxury branding is taken here, to include intangible identity brands, small enterprize brands, as well as the more traditional sense of branded material commodities that can be bought and sold directly. This approach is well-established in the critical literature on luxury (Armitage and Roberts, 2016a; 2016b; Batat, 2019; Berry, 1994) and branding (Holt, 2002, 2004; Okonkwo, 2016).

On most of the continent, smartphones and mobile phone internet connections are the main way that people get online (David and Grobler, 2020). Consequently, economic activity online and facilitated by digital forms of communication are also growing – from the context-specific e-commerce company Jumia, finally turning a profit after almost ten years of operation (Bright, 2020), to the flowering of micro-stores selling their wares through social media pages, to platforms that facilitate new ways to book, buy, and sell, without a doubt internet penetration in Africa is linked to economic activity and growth (see for example Ndemo and Weiss, 2016). Some even argue that the presence of the internet can reduce inequality (Asongu and Odhiambo, 2019) – though of course the ways in which technology also reproduces power relations must not be ignored (Gagliardone, 2016). Regardless, in Africa as elsewhere, the marketing of luxury goods happens significantly in the palm of the hand, scrolling on Instagram, and other social media sites (but especially Instagram). Instagram is an extremely popular social media site (Leaver et al., 2020), especially for visual communication, and it has developed a certain resonance with luxury branding and lifestyles (Caldeira, 2020; Iqani, 2018; Marwick, 2015). It has been tipped as a key platform for visual communication in Africa (Becker, 2016).

For these reasons, Instagram provides the main source of promotional communications and brand imaging discussed in the book. Like luxury brands everywhere, African labels have their own websites and formal offline advertising communications (including store fronts, magazine features, and events). In the age of cross-platform, intertextual branding (Hardy, 2010), it is no surprise that these other forms of promotional communication converge into social media posts, with the Instagram grid functioning as a curated repository for all the relevant communications that brands may wish to archive. Methodologically, this book considers how luxury brand messages converge on Instagram, with consideration given to the movement of discourse and ideas between brands and in their collaborations, on and offline, where relevant. Key case studies of iconic images shared by important brands are analysed and discussed in detail in order to advance critical analysis of promotional communications in African contexts. Analytical approaches from critical (Schroeder, 2002, 2007) and decolonial (Disemelo, 2019a; Tamale, 2020) visual analysis and multimodal discourse analysis (Jewitt, 2009; Kress, 2013; Kress and Leeuwen, 2001) are deployed in order to show how the African luxury brands use specific cultural meanings, and also push forward transgressive understandings of luxury in African contexts.

Alongside the Instagram material, I also purposively collected publicly available media materials about luxury in other media platforms, including mainstream newspapers and magazine articles and relevant trade publications. Of course there was often an overlap between the content on Instagram, the physical world of the retail spaces and interview settings, and the comments and statements of my interview participants. In some ways it was the media content itself that provided the conduit through which the other data were connected. It is extremely rare for a brand to not have an Instagram presence, and this is perhaps particularly true for luxury brands. Furthermore, those working in the sector seem to be expected to have a strong social media presence by their employers, or actively establish one themselves for entrepreneurial purposes. Luxury retail spaces too, need to be active on the platform, and across all these iterations of luxury in individual people, retail brands, commodities, and practices, there is an accompanying highly visual media narrative archived and organized by hashtag and featuring feedback and comments from viewers. As such, Instagram is both a living library and a valuable repository of texts that communicate ideas about luxury, which are often linked to and repeated in other spaces and conversations. All of the brands analysed in this book are active on Instagram, and have public profiles in which they post content that is explicitly intended for wide public consumption. Permission has been secured where possible, to reproduce the images that I include, but I argue that all of them are fair use on the basis of having been explicitly posted with the intention of being made public by those who own them, who wished for them to be widely seen and discussed.

Being with and in Luxury: Ethnographic Approaches

The analysis of brand-created material presented in this book is undergirded and contextualized with ethnographic work. It is well established in critical research on consumer culture that ethnographic approaches (Healy et al., 2007; Sherry et al., 2001) are key to examining the textures of lived experience as well as the particular cultural geographies of promotional cultures. My ethnographic work to examine and experience luxury cultures in African cities comprised field visits to Cape Town, Accra, Nairobi, Lagos, and Kampala, as well as ongoing events-based observation in my own home city of Johannesburg. My empirical work was limited to African countries that use English as a key language, as my linguistic capacities do not extend to Francophone or Lusophone settings. Further, I kept my focus on sub-Saharan Africa, as arguably

Arabic-speaking North African countries have unique regional characteristics not shared with the rest of the continent. I also limited my work to major cities, as these are typically the epicentre of luxury promotional culture in each country. My empirical work took place over three years, from 2017 to 2019. On a prosaic level, this involved visiting and being in luxury spaces: "hanging out" in luxurious hotel lobbies, strolling the glittering walkways of high end malls, window shopping in luxury boutiques, gaining access, where possible, to events promoting luxury brands, and spending time sitting and writing in fancy cafés while drinking cappuccinos and people watching. While this may sound to some like leisure, not research, I have no doubt that the immersion in luxury spaces and settings in various African cities has contributed in significant ways to my understanding of how luxury is shaped and deployed, and how it takes on specific meanings that circulate through popular culture. Of course, as the ethnographic mindset requires, I strived to be reflexive in my observational work, and to be mindful of my own positionality in relation to the spaces and places that I frequented. This required remaining mindful of my racial, gender, and class positionalities throughout.

Although my ethnic background is mixed, comprising of Middle Eastern and English heritages, in South Africa, where I was raised but not born, I was classified white and am read that way by some, although not all, of my fellow citizens. (It is not unusual for me to be asked pointed questions about my racial "category" or ethnicity by students, personnel in municipal offices, bank tellers, or new acquaintances: "what *are* you?"). When travelling elsewhere on the continent, when asked where I am from I always say South Africa. In Lagos, I might look Lebanese-Nigerian, in Nairobi and Kampala I might be taken for a South Asian East African. But what unites these experiences of my positionality in the African luxury milieu is that I am not a Black African, and despite the existence of racial and cultural diversity in every African nation, cross-generational and forged by new immigrants and temporary visitors, I am an outsider, even in the land of my own upbringing. From the ethnographic perspective, the condition of being an outsider is useful, as it allows a sense of curiosity and critical distance (Hammersley and Atkinson, 1995), a more careful approach to looking and seeing. Having been raised in Africa, and having had the opportunity to travel relatively widely in the continent since I was a child, I am not an outsider in quite the same way that a first-time white visitor to Lagos, Accra, or Kampala might be. I am something of a conditional insider, someone who knows African cities and towns relatively well, having for all but five years of my life lived in them and visited them. As both and neither an outsider nor insider, as someone who identifies as at-once English, African, and Middle-Eastern, my liminal ethnicity and personal experiences with the continent offer an opportunity to reach for a balance between critical distance and uncritical celebration. I strive to engage both my sense of proximity to African cities, and my status as someone who does not fully belong, in the analytical work shared in this book. Similarly, I acknowledge that my race and class have afforded me privilege. The class privileges attached to whiteness in African contexts often marked me as belonging to the consumer cultures I was studying, even though in practice I am not at all a connoisseur of luxury items. Elsewhere I have written on reflexivity in luxury research, showing how proximity to highly expensive lifestyles affected me as a researcher in crucial ways, and offering a theory of reflexive positioning in relation to luxury for other researchers to consider (Iqani, 2022).

Alongside observational work, and maintaining reflexivity in relation to both context and luxury, I undertook interviews with fifty workers in the African luxury sector. None of the interview participants cited in this book worked for the brands whose communications are analysed in this book. In each chapter, I bring interview material into the discussion to develop an argument or provide context. This contributes to a well-established body of work that aims to critically understand the operations of marketers and advertisers as an important site of cultural production (Ariztia, 2013; Cronin, 2004; Mazzarella, 2003; Nixon, 2003). I have written elsewhere about how branding and marketing professionals active in the luxury sector in Anglophone African cities talk about the work that they do, including how they engage with social media marketing, influencers (Iqani, 2021), gendered ideas of their markets (Iqani, In Press), and the importance of their sector socially and ethically. I include further details about the interview process and participants in Appendix 1.

I followed most of my interview participants on Instagram, as well as brands relevant to their work, and through this extended my understanding of not only conversations about luxury, but also who was involved in it. An extended participant observation of content and engagement about luxury in African contexts took place in parallel with the "real-world" ethnographic work and the interviews. This involved viewing, saving and sometimes engaging with content created and shared by my interview participants and other key players in the African luxury sector whom I did not speak to directly. Online material often-times informed interviews; I would refer to a specific Instagram post or profile when asking a question, or participants would mention someone I should follow. At times, media practices were the direct subject of conversation, when I asked participants to tell me more about how they used social media to promote their brands or do their work, at other times this subject matter was more implicit.

For this book, I have integrated material from interviews and ethnographic observation with the analyses of brand content. For want of a better term, the data from all three sources were triangulated, less to validate veracity, and more to knit together a more complex and nuanced picture of key aspects of brand communications. My intention is both to show how online and offline discourses are intricately connected (in relation to luxury specifically but also in relation to mediated culture broadly), as well as to give full justice to the complexity and interrelatedness of the state of luxury promotional culture in African contexts.

Structure of the Book

This chapter has, so far, set the scene by empirically and theoretically bringing together ideas from critical literature on branding (Aronczyk and Powers, 2010; Arvidsson, 2005), African and diaspora studies (Azevedo, 2018), decolonial theory (Dei and Lordan, 2016; Mignolo and Walsh, 2018), and critical race theory (Crenshaw et al., 1995; Treviño et al., 2008). It has shown how African luxury branding extends, but also complicates, global neoliberal culture. Until recently, in the global imaginary Africa has commonly been stereotyped as backward and poverty stricken. A new narrative of Africa and Africans as "rising" (Amankwah-Amoah et al., 2018; Bunce et al., 2016; Taylor, 2014) has started to gain dominance, especially in what some have summarized as the "Wakanda moment," in reference to the massive popular success of the 2018 film *Black Panther* (Carrington, 2019; Coetzee, 2019). Partly as a result of the cultural power of the African-American cultural and creative industries, and the rise of global awareness of the Black Lives Matter movement, including the trending of key images and messages on social media platforms globally (Sobande, 2019), African aesthetics are present, more complexly than ever, in global media discourses. These reach consumer markets in various, interrelated contexts: local and regional affluent Africans, members of the Diaspora, and a broader multi-cultural global audience.

The remainder of this book presents three themed analytical chapters, followed by a theoretical concluding chapter. The empirical chapters each have a similar structure. Chosen brand case studies are presented and contextualized, and iconic images from their branding campaigns are analysed and theorized, with relevant ethnographic and interview material brought in to develop and assist the analysis. Each chapter ends with a concluding discussion that brings together case study material into a synthetic presentation of new theory. The chapters are organized around specific themes, and case studies selected to speak to and from those themes. The first theme is *Culture*, which is perhaps the most recognizable luxury sensibility to be captured by African brands. Chapter 2 explores how indigenous aesthetics and inheritances are presented and remixed by luxury brands, into a global message that functions as a form of soft power. The second theme is *Nature*. In Chapter 3, I show how an earthy minimalism takes shape and is deployed in some African luxury brands: eschewing stereotyped animal print volubility in favour of neutral minerality and quiet plant-based aesthetics. I show how this is linked to the politics of Black feminism. The third theme explored is *Future*: in Chapter 4 the focus shifts to powerful avant-garde creatives that centre a queer sensibility of shine that pushes well beyond culture and nature to produce entirely original, forward-looking aesthetics that are at once African and quintessentially global.

Throughout this book, the argument is made that luxury is a crucial modality through which time is discursively transcended, as it allows for both a reaching into the past to find and reclaim narratives of authenticity and a surging into the future as it offers a highly optimistic narrative about economic growth and the realization of hopes and dreams for better quality, more beautiful, more authentic, aesthetically meaningful lives. The unique contribution of this book is the claim that for Africa and Africans, luxury is crucial to the politics of the good life. Taking this seriously allows critical cultural theorists to advance our work on the meanings of consumption in an increasingly unequal world.

2 From Africa to the World: Cultural Inheritance as Soft Power

This chapter explores luxury brands that capitalize on indigenous African cultural aesthetics. It shows how narratives of cultural inheritance are one key feature of the discourse of African luxury presented to markets around the world. First, using interview data, I show the centrality of the narrative of authenticity to African luxury branding. Then, with the help of two case studies, I argue that the claiming of specific forms of cultural authenticity and inheritance is a key form of soft power, which African creatives are leveraging in order to claim a place within the global luxury marketplace. This allows them to re-present the value of African creativity and to capitalize on processes of commodifying heritage resources. The chapter concludes by critically theorizing how African luxury soft power illuminates the politics of cultural capitalism.

Authenticity in Luxury Design

The notion of authenticity is central to the definition of a brand or product as luxurious (Morhart and Malär, 2020; Septianto et al., 2020). Authenticity is a familiar trope in the management literature on luxury, and it is often signposted as one of the most important indicators of a luxury brand. The notion of an authentic cultural heritage concerns how long a brand has been around but also how it has refined its craft over that time. Further, it points to the legitimacy of a brand's claim to owning and representing some unique cultural aspect. In the context of European fashion houses, for example, that authenticity is expressed through narratives about the history of tailoring clothing or distilling cognac in a particular region or even family. A sense of history having been somehow captured in the elite and unique material practices of a particular luxury brand is one of the key selling points.

DOI: 10.4324/9781003227038-2

In African contexts, luxury is often associated with newness by outside commentators. In Chapter 1, I showed how it is problematic that African luxury consumers are termed "new" by global commentators, as though they have only just been born into consumer identities, and as though they are in need of education in the correct and appropriate ways to desire and access luxury goods. This problematic, indeed racist, notion that Africans need educating in the values of luxury was utterly ignored by the luxury workers that I interviewed. Instead, they spoke to the power and pleasures of connecting with their own cultural histories of craftsmanship and luxury, and the expert labour required to bring those narratives into their business and communicative practices. Indeed, elite material practices and luxurious aesthetic forms have always been part of a wide variety of African cultures, and many contemporary African luxury entrepreneurs are committed to excavating these, and presenting them to the global marketplace of ideas as having equal value to the historical narratives of luxury emanating from the West. Many African luxury entrepreneurs are keenly aware of the interest that wealthy and upwardly mobile African consumers have in African aesthetics and brands.

> Africa is so vibrant, so dynamic, such an infusion of different things and there's something quite unique about it. I think of my own culture and how I pay quite a bit of money to revisit things that I didn't care about in my youth. We've already got clients that are willing to pay for *a version of luxury that belongs to us* that we've forgotten or never connected with (Lerato – emphasis added).

As Lerato, a luxury entrepreneur and consultant in South Africa, puts it, African consumers are actively looking for beautiful, luxurious objects that belong to their identities and personal cultural affiliations. In our discussion, she explicitly pointed out that African luxury brands are not interested in mimicking the narratives of European brands. Rather, they have, "a better story to tell." African luxury brands can and do capitalize on the "version of luxury that belongs to us."

Bella, a designer working in east Africa, articulates this opportunity as a "point of authenticity." African consumers want to buy beautiful things that are culturally meaningful in a personal way, but also to the cultures of other Africans across the continent. They do not want to buy these beautiful things from non-African brands, even as global brands are eyeing the African market or appropriating African aesthetics (Feldman, 2017). Bella argues that African luxury brands have an opportunity to "fill that gap" – growing consumer aspirations for luxury products that feel relevant to and emerge from African contexts and cultures – "before the flood comes in" – Africanized commodities and marketing from global brands. Now that Africans have more money, she explains, African luxury brands need to do the entrepreneurial and communicative work to show their potential consumers that "we've been here all the time because we appreciate you." Bella is explaining both the challenge and the opportunity of the moment: African consumers are desiring more luxury, and before global brands swoop in to sell those items to them, African luxury brands should establish themselves as the more authentic and trustworthy options, because they are *truly* African, and they encompass all the best and most beautiful things that African cultures have to offer.

Remixing Cultural Heritage into Luxury Objects

In order to explore the role of cultural heritage in African luxury branding, I work with two case studies of luxury brands that explicitly call upon specific narratives of cultural heritage in their branding and design work. The first is the eponymous The be Magugu, an haute couture fashion brand founded in 2017, and the second is jewellery line, The Herd, which was founded by Mbali Mthethwa in 2018. Each brand centres narratives and aesthetics that explicitly draw on Sotho and Zulu history and tradition respectively, and repurposes those cultural materials into luxury commodities.

From Rites to Runways: Thebe Magugu and the Basotho Blanket

Thebe Magugu is an haute couture designer gaining fame and recognition across the world. Magugu hails from Kimberly, a small town in the Northern Cape of South Africa, which is likely the last town many South Africans would name as the country's fashion capital. Nevertheless, his oeuvre is wide and growing, and each collection seems to achieve more adulation and praise from fashion lovers than the last. Thebe Magugu has been worn by high profile celebrities in South Africa and abroad, including Issa Rae, Miley Cyrus, and Dionne Warwick. The brand-designer was a finalist in the LVMH Prize in 2019. The aesthetic of the collections is avant garde, drawing on eclectic references, but Magugu is specific to elucidate when he references his own cultural heritage in his design work. For the purposes of this chapter, I wish to focus on one garment: Magugu's reinterpretation of the Basotho blanket, which is named the "Basotho

Poncho." In an Instagram post on 13 January 2021, Thebe Magugu states, along with photographer credits:

> The Basotho Poncho is inspired by my Sotho cultural heritage, made of Cotton Jacquard grown and spun in South Africa.
>
> (@thebemagugu)

This simple message accompanies a series of four photographs. The first three show the Basotho Poncho from front, side, and back (see Figure 2.1 for front and back view). The fourth photograph shows an anthropological photo of a gathering of young Basotho initiates, wearing the blankets that are the original reference point for Magugu's design. The Instagram images featuring the Poncho show a tall slim model with a sculptural afro in the shape of an eye. She stands on a large overturned white plastic washtub, in front of a crisp white sheet attached to a clothes line with three white pegs, hanging perfectly and geometrically straight behind her. The white sheet offers a pristine framing for the model, with the ensemble placed in front of a slightly dimmer white infinity curve. The model wears striking thigh-high ruffled red suede boots, and under the poncho one of Magugu's sculptural white shirt dresses, its double wrap pussy-bow tie suggesting

(a)   (b)

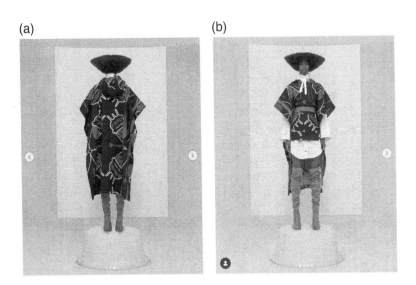

Figure 2.1 Thebe Magugu's Basotho Poncho, front and back view from Instagram post. Reproduced with permission of Thebe Magugu. Photography by Travys Owen.

a jabot spilling out from the collar. The poncho itself is dark blue with white printed motifs of a three-legged cast iron cooking pot and forks, and red graphic stripes along one shoulder. The front of the poncho sits at hip level, it's wide sleeves ending at the elbow. The second image in the series shows the garment from the side, where its silhouette shows an elegant sweep from front to back, and a hood. The third image in the series shows the poncho from the back, where it is revealed as reaching beyond the back of the knees, and the full pattern of the interspersed *potjes* is displayed, embellished by the stripes, both important motifs often present on Basotho blanket designs.

Basotho blankets are highly recognizable artefacts, which outsiders observe to be a special feature of the culture. The Basotho blanket has been the object of much anthropological fascination. The key point is that in Basotho culture blankets are not used simply to sleep under or to stay warm, they are worn in various significant ways, and their wearing and gifting is central to important spiritual and family occasions. Indeed the blanket is so central to various forms of mourning and celebration, and to indicate social relationships, cultural status, life stage and community connections, it has been said that in Basotho culture, "the blanket is life" (Bosko, 1981: 23). As well as being beautiful, Basotho blankets are heavy, wind resistant, and famously warm, shielding the wearer from any chill (including the high altitude, frigid winds of the Lesotho mountains). Their symbolism goes well beyond that protection. Blankets are an extremely important cultural objects for people of Sotho heritage. Blankets figure in important life occasions including birth, marriage, homecomings, initiation transitions to adulthood, and death (Bosko, 1981; Pheto-Moeti, 2020). Basotho blankets are pure wool, and feature a number of stylized and immediately recognizable designs, for example, the spear and shield, the three-legged cast iron cooking pot already seen on Magugu's poncho, an aloe that grows only in the Lesotho highlands, and the motifs from a deck of playing cards (clubs, aces, diamonds, and hearts). Although they are intimately linked with Basotho culture, the blankets were introduced by British colonialists (Pheto-Moeti, 2020), and are manufactured at the Aranda factory in Krugersdorp (Mason, 2017) in the West Rand gold belt (now empty of gold) near Johannesburg, and then distributed across the country to Basotho communities in the Free State and over the border into Lesotho, the "mountain kingdom" landlocked within South Africa's territory (and entirely economically dependent on it).

Along with many other traditional forms of attire recognizable from across the African continent, the Basotho blanket was made globally famous by the styling of the character W'Kabi, played by Daniel

Kaluuya, in *Black Panther* (2018). W'Kabi is a friend and advisor to the Black Panther and is a prince of the "Border Tribe," tasked with defending Wakanda from external threats. In the film he wears two kinds of blankets, which borrow heavily from the iconic look of Basotho herdsmen, who drape their blankets elegantly, fixed at the shoulder. W'Kabi's iconic, and perhaps most recognizable outfit features a blanket with special protective powers, blue with inlaid "metallic foil printed designs" (https://www.blackpanthercostu.me/ wkabi-the-border-tribe/) and a Basotho style black and white pattern on the interior. In key "court" and "ceremony" scenes of the film, chorus ensembles of men and women wrapped in Basotho blankets are also notable (see Becker, 2019). Black Panther played a huge role in mainstreaming a diversity of African aesthetics into the global imagination, spurred on by the powerful African-American cultural industry, and indeed presenting utopian images of Afro-futurism and decolonization (Becker, 2019). The impact that this in turn may have had in highlighting the creative work of African fashion designers is significant. The acclaimed, Oscar-winning work of Ruth E. Carter in the costume design for *Black Panther* can be seen as making a strong contribution to global black pride and the aesthetics of "Africanicity" (Dosekun, 2019), which is mediated in significant ways through luxury fashion. Read as such, the Basotho blanket is not appropriated by African-American Hollywood culture, but celebrated and catapulted into a new spotlight of appreciation.

The French luxury brand Louis Vuitton used the aesthetics of the Basotho blanket in their Spring-Summer 2017 runway collection, which included an outfit made of fabric "displaying designs of giraffes, palm leaves, corn cups and four pinstripes, produced with a matching shirt" (Lunde, 2019: 7). Big luxury brands like Louis Vuitton see the entire world of cultural expression as theirs to use in any way they wish, but arguably there is something problematic in their blatant – some might say blatantly unimaginative – reproduction of the blue and yellow corn-motif of one of the most recognizable designs of Basotho blankets, not even pausing to remix the pattern into something slightly more original, and even including one of the actual blankets, priced at $2000 (they ordinarily sell for around $200), in the ensemble (Lunde, 2019: 8). Fashion designers consider themselves artists and draw on a wide range of aesthetic materials from a wide range of cultures for inspiration. When white and western designers "borrow" the Basotho blanket for their own collections, it should be considered cultural appropriation, even though the nuances of how the borrowing is done is a key aspect of the debate. Simply "shifting culturally anchored" designs from one context to another is problematic, especially if there was a lack of genuine intercultural interaction (Chatterjee, 2020: 53). Cultural appropriation is particularly egregious when profit accrues to the appropriator (Lenard and Balint, 2020: 331). In the LV case, it has been concluded by Kristin Lunde that the brand was not appropriating Basotho culture, only "appreciating" it (Lunde, 2019), though not all may agree with this. It is important to bear in mind that the playing field of fashion design is not level, and that the highly successful, profitable western brands are working with economies of scale and scope and already well-established markets that African designers may not yet have the resources to compete with. With this in mind, when an actual Sotho fashion designer uses the Basotho blanket as a resource in their creative practice, it is important to pause to consider the politics of this aesthetic choice, and its presentation as part of a rightful cultural inheritance.

Returning to the Basotho Poncho pictured in Figure 2.1, it is very important that Thebe Magugu points out in his caption that the item is inspired by his *own* cultural heritage. Having Sesotho blood and ancestry gives him a special positionality in which taking and using the Basotho blanket as a reference point in his design is not only justifiable but ethical. Magugu has done more than simply take the blanket and use it in an ensemble, like Louis Vuitton did. He has reimagined it and presented an entirely original garment – the poncho – even though it offers a recognizably Basotho blanket look and feel. By so doing, Magugu presents an original argument: that if any designer has a right to take and reimagine certain aspects of Basotho cultural heritage, it is a designer with Sotho blood themselves. It is worth pausing to consider the way in which Magugu has phrased his creative intervention, as *inspired* by his own heritage. Rather than simply taking an existing item from another culture, he has re-configured something from his own in such a way as to make it completely new, with key aspects of the original form remaining recognizable. The colour palette of the poncho remains true to Basotho tradition: blue and white are key colours in the blankets, as is the red stripe which is a recurring feature of many of the blanket designs. Further, the symbolism of the three-legged pot is poignant, referring to off-the-grid, rural cooking. This nod to a pre-modern idyllic is echoed in the styling of the photo, with the model standing on the washtub used in rural living to wash clothes and bathe bodies. The integration of rural symbolism with high fashion is not new, but it is very successful in the image. Pairing a blanket-like wrap with thigh-high red stiletto boots is precisely the kind of juxtaposition, bringing divergent but complementary sensibilities into dialogue with one another, that makes fashion exciting. It is however important that the visual thrills produced by the wide-ranging and eclectic sampling that fashion designers employ have an artistic integrity underlying the surface aesthetic. Although cultural integrity is not the only way to secure a deeper level of meaning and authenticity in fashion artistry, in this case it is a key strategy. I will come back to this in the final section of this chapter. Next though, I offer another intriguing case study in the presentation of indigenous aesthetics in luxury design.

The Love Language of Beads: The Herd

The Herd is a luxury beading company started by Mbali Mthethwa in 2018. The company "is inspired by and pays homage to the iconic beading cultures pioneered and mastered by Nguni women" (www.theherddesigns.com/about). The Nguni are a cultural group comprising of Zulu, Xhosa, Ndebele, and Swazi cultures, and make up nearly two-thirds of South Africa's Black African population (https://www.sahistory.org.za/article/zulu). As will become clear, the particular style of beading used by this brand is most strongly linked to Zulu cultural history.

The Herd necklaces (see Figure 2.2) draw on a long tradition of communicative beading in Nguni cultures, but reinterprets the aesthetic into a highly contemporary design sensibility. The necklaces are hand-made and limited edition and feature a flat decorative surface,

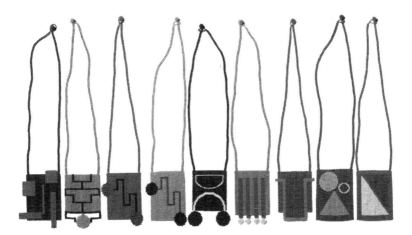

Figure 2.2 Necklace collection, © The Herd, Reproduced with kind permission of Mbali Mthethwa.

often square or rectangular, that sits against the sternum of the wearer, connected with a thin double-beaded filament that hangs around the neck. Although various forms of beaded necklaces have been part of cultural expression in Southern Africa for centuries (Nettleton, 2015), The Herd positions itself as design, without disassociating from the artisanal skill required to individually hand-bead the pieces. Indeed, the handiwork and skilful artistry of the process is at the centre of the story told by the brand. Each necklace is woven with a carefully chosen colour palette and offers an abstract geometric patterning that is at once symbolic and decorative. Against the pixel-work of the woven bead texture, circles, stripes, and triangles are integrated, both within the frame of the decorative part, and innovatively extruding from it.

In the dynamic juxtaposition of simple shapes and lines, a unique aesthetic sensibility emerges. Beadwork requires each individual tiny bead to occupy its place in an intentionally conceptualized grid of colour, weaving them together so as to produce a coherent pattern or image. Although abstract, the patterns of The Herd necklaces suggest movement and a relationship developing between the graphic elements of each design. Figure 2.2 shows the image included as a header on The Herd's web store (https://theherddesigns.com/neckpieces). Each necklace offers multiple possible associations and interpretations. For example, the piece second from the right could be read as sun and moon over a mountain or a conversation between three deities, while the third and fourth pieces from the left could be read as cityscapes or map-routes connecting origin with destination on land or sea. The piece third from the left could be read as arms supplicating heavenwards, or as a receptacle filled with some form of nourishment. These are just two possible interpretations for the visual components of each necklace; the point is that they are ripe with symbolism, and they invite the viewer and wearer to imagine the stories they are telling. The necklaces serve as both a bold style statement for their wearer, and as subtle suggestions of any number of emotive messages. "Beadwork has no life without the body that wears and animates it; as the body moves the light plays across and off the surface of the beads" (Nettleton, 2009: 3); it is therefore significant that the pieces are intended to be worn. As embodied, decorative luxury items that carry a multiplicity of symbolisms, the Herd necklaces are animated by human subjectivity and phenomenology.

Mbali Mthethwa, the brand's founder and designer, emphasizes on the website and Instagram postings that The Herd's artistic intention is to revive the under-valued art of beading as a form of communication, and to celebrate the aesthetic and cultural power of beading as a love language, in particular. The deep symbolism associated with different geometric forms – circles, triangles, rectangles – have specific meaning and spiritual resonance in Nguni cultures, and The Herd beaders are doubtless drawing on ancestral understandings and unique cultural associations, but when they are encoded into the necklaces, which then become available in elite fashion stores or are drooled over by Instagram fans, those meanings are opened up to a variety of interpretations. Zulu beading has been the object of historical, anthropological, and visual arts study, with scholars pointing out the various iconographic and cultural meanings of the practice and objects produced (Nettleton, 2015; Xulu, 2002). By speaking of beading as a "love language," Mthethwa is explicitly linking her brand with the tradition of "Zulu Love Letters" (Biyela, 2013a, 2013b), a traditional communications practice among Zulu communities in which women would "create a beaded message with rainbow colours to engage the recipient's mind" during courtship with a suitor (Biyela, 2013a: 38). In this context, beading is a language that is deployed as a form of relationship building and affective romance, where the communicative resource is "a combination of arrangement of colours of beads" (Biyela, 2013a: 39), with different colours and shapes sending specific messages at each point in a couple's romance.

I would like to put the aesthetic and ethic of The Herd's reconfigured, modernized "love letters" into dialogue with the critically acclaimed film, co-written by Bhekizizwe Peterson and directed by Ramadan Suleman, *Zulu Love Letter* (2004). This film tells the story of a woman journalist who witnessed the murder of an anti-apartheid activist by the apartheid government's secret police, and who struggles, understandably, to recover from this trauma once South African democracy dawns. A key visual motif of the film is the "love letter" (a multimedia tapestry art project) that the protagonist's deaf, estranged daughter is making for her mother, as an attempt to cross the growing divide between them. The daughter's art project serves as powerful symbol of how many individuals have struggled to cope with the social, emotional, and psychological scars of the inter-generational trauma caused by apartheid's vicious oppressions and human rights abuses. As the screenwriter (also important South African cultural theorist) Bhekizizwe Peterson explains, the film's "love letter" "encapsulates the therapeutic role of the arts and their capacity to foster love and healing through memory work" (Peterson, 2009: 24). The beadwork necklace, "a long-established indigenous creative practice" serves as a "modern narrative device" allowing the film to "propel an engaging personal and public story of the South African experience in a different medium" (Cham, 2009: x). In other words, the "love letter" is a metaphor for the centrality of creative communication for healing historical pain and trauma. At the same time, the "love letter" also celebrates and honours cultural heritage and creativity.

The Herd necklaces perform similar work, albeit more modestly than the complex multimodal components of the feature film form. Each The Herd necklace also "engages an African aesthetics rooted in an African spirituality" (Maingard, 2009: 5). Borrowing Bhekizizwe Peterson's concept of "interludes" (a filmic device that allows the boundaries of past and present to be visually bridged) (Maingard, 2009: 12), I read The Herd's bead necklaces as a communicative mode that visually stitches together sensibilities from the past and contemporary fashion. Because they are hand woven and crafted, they carry with them the sensibilities of the hands that made them, and the generations of women before who nurtured and guided those hands. In their beauty there is also heart: a celebration of this particular form of creation, and the cultural resonance that it carries, as well as the particular set of messages encoded within each necklace. For example, one limited-edition range from The Herd is called, *isimo somhlaba* (the condition of the land). It,

> is inspired by one of the first bead excavations that were discovered in uMgungundlovu, which was the capital of the Zulu kingdom during the reign of King Dingane. The beads excavated relate to the period 1828–1839. Reading up on these excavations inspired us to imagine what the landscape looked like then (https://convoyshop. co/collections/the-herd/products/large-letters).

The particular range of necklaces to which this description refers feature abstract geometric "maps," which to those unaware of the specific history Mthethwa is referencing, will simply read as beautiful patterns. Yet they also encode a rewriting of history, that is arguably highly therapeutic for those doing the beading and the re-telling of these stories of the beaders who came before them. The beads from today, and the beads excavated from 200 years ago are part of the same history and culture, not linear but inter-stitched across time with a strong recognition of inter-generational ancestry throughout. Peterson writes that his film was created as a "love letter to those who passed on and those still tasked with creating a better future for all" (Peterson, 2021). Mbali Mthethwa is part of a new generation of creatives who look to the past – and not just any past, but their own cultural histories wounded and marginalized by the racist power of apartheid – to excavate modalities for telling stories that resonate with the present, both to offer healing and to preserve important forms of cultural expression for posterity. The Herd could be read as one version of creative practice that reincarnates the complex ethics and aesthetics of inter-generational healing explored in *Zulu Love Letter*.

Traditionally in Zulu culture, the art and craft of beading is women's specialty, and this is emphasized and celebrated in The Herd's communications. The practice of beading threads together ancestry and history with contemporary luxury sensibilities. Mthethwa emphasizes, on the Herd's website the linking together of an older generation of skilled women bead-artists with the millennial, urban, fashionable aesthetes who buy her necklaces. In this way, she also bridges certain boundaries, bringing together past and present through the modality of beading and the stories contained within those colours and patterns. By exploring historical narratives of culture, feminism and the aesthetic of beading and stitching these together into very contemporary luxury commodities that intentionally tell specific stories of legacy and cultural inheritance, The Herd is also performing an act of communicating across the boundaries of time, with and through specific cultural heritage that was maligned and marginalized by apartheid. In pre-colonial African cultures, beads were a prestige item, especially in the Zulu Kingdom, and beadwork was "at once public because it was worn to be seen, and private, because it was made by an individual woman for someone of significance to her" (Nettleton, 2009: 1). Beadwork always also contained a sense of the future, because it "conveyed aspects of the young woman's wishes, hopes and dreams" (Nettleton, 2009: 2). In this sense, The Herd necklaces also function as inter-generational love letters, that reach back into the past as well as into the future, through the luxurious sensibility of hand-made woven beadwork, that is "historically rooted and yet modern" and thus able to signal "an imaginary, contested, contemporary African community" (Nettleton, 2009: 3).

Luxury Design across Time and Space

The two creative modalities of the brands discussed here – the weave of the blanket and beading, respectively – both rely upon a particular visual form that is comprised of many tiny components arranged together aesthetically. In textiles, two or more threads that form a unit is called a "block," and these can be arranged in an almost limitless number of patterns and forms, allowing them to serve as a rich resource for artistry. Similarly, in beading each individual glass bead serves as the unit from which patterns are only limited by the artist's imagination. Both weaving and beading can be compared with pixel art, where each pixel is the building block for any number of images and designs. The artisanal forms of weaving and beading have a direct aesthetic connection to modern computational communication. The "block" units and beads are each a pixel, and the art created with blocks and beads is simulated when pixels are intentionally and artfully arranged. Human creativity and ingenuity links traditional artisanal forms of communication with computer aided communication. The units, be they beads, blocks, or pixels, serve as the raw material for the creation of beautiful things. And these units stretch across time, as analogue forms of communication that have been used in human culture, from past to present, as a unifying modality of human creative expression.

Both brands – Thebe Magugu and The Herd – reach back across time to retrieve particular cultural resources that are reinscribed into contemporary aesthetics. Drawing on Bheki Peterson's (Maingard, 2009) notion of the "interlude" – a narrative device that bridges between past and present, I argue that the Basotho Poncho and bead necklace are more than mere luxury commodities, as beautiful and desirable as both are. They are also channels of communication that speak to loss and recovery, to pride and also a gendered sense of belonging. From the perspective of Magugu, the claim to belonging in and with Basotho cultural heritage is mediated through a particular narrative of spiritual and cultural significance, linked to the ancestors, rooted in the rites of cultural belonging (Figure 2.3).

The physical garb of the post-initiation clothing – remediated here as a luxury African brand, made by and for one's own – both stands in for the finery of the pre-colonial masculinity initiation rites, where young men would wear special blankets to signal their maturity, and presents that finery as something non-Sotho others can access and integrate into their self-styling as a modern resource. Because it is being offered into the global luxury fashion market by Thebe Magugu himself, the problematics of cultural appropriation, although not entirely removed, are dampened down, and all customers are welcomed to engage with, and consume, the cultural resources being redeployed through the brand. Heritage implies history, and in the (South) African context, in which colonialism and racist violence brutalized Black African people, including through the degradation of their cultural aesthetics and practices, it is a powerful move to reclaim and celebrate those resources. Equally, there is power in remixing those

Figure 2.3 Basotho initiates, Thebe Magugu's reference for his Basotho Poncho. Photograph © David M. M. Riep and reproduced with his kind permission.

resources into a new aesthetic that appeals both to members of that cultural group and outsiders. Were Magugu to limit himself to wishing to sell his garments to Sotho customers only, he would immediately miss a huge potential market. The artfulness of how Magugu has balanced the task of staying true to his reading of the values of

Basotho culture with presenting an aesthetic that draws on it without caricaturing it but instead presenting a highly original aesthetic that is intelligible as fashion to customers around the world, is key. Notably, the striking blanket patterns that Magugu re-mediates into the poncho maintain a sense of cultural authenticity *and* transcend it. Although the image of the initiates is dated as having been taken in 2010, it suggests a deeper history. The anthropological framing of Basotho initiates seems to reach back in time, to take us away from the modern and towards the traditional, as suggested by the intimate framing of the young men standing with heads bowed, faces and scalps ochre-painted, hair combed into beautiful patterns, draped in their initiation blankets. The modern and traditional are not binary opposites but are integrated in complex ways, with traditional objects like the blanket remaining important to the spiritual rites and customs of African indigenous cultures today. Magugu re-mediates the blanket into the poncho, keeping recognizable elements such as the draping, colour-palette, patterning, and vertical stripe, yet exchanging wool for jacquard cotton, and the changeable blanket for the fixed silhouette of the hooded poncho. And in so doing, he reaches into the past for resources that are made newly relevant to the present.

The Herd also reaches back across time to reclaim, and remediate, a specific cultural practice. Love letters – be they Zulu or other – can be theorized as media forms that cross time and space, carrying messages from one to another through a specific arrangement of communicative resources. The power of this communicative form extends well beyond the sender and receiver, it also works across cultures and centuries. As Mthethwa explains in the Instagram post reproduced in Figure 2.4, the skill of beading is passed down from generation to generation, a practice that connects the past with the present. The images showing the hands of the master beader at work celebrate the beauty of Black skin, but also carry the lines and stories of the beader's particular life story, as well as the bigger narrative of cultural heritage that she is passing on through her artwork. The artisanal craft of the hand-beading is a practice taught by mothers to daughters, and as such must be understood as an inter-generational cultural resource, indeed, an important method – akin to language preservation – of keeping a culture alive. Beading is an art form, and also a way of telling stories with hands and hearts, with images and objects. These are stories not simply of individuals and their romantic intentions towards one another, but also stories of place and time, of culture and heritage. Again, as is the case with Thebe Magugu, The Herd mines a specific cultural heritage (with which it's owner and founder closely identifies

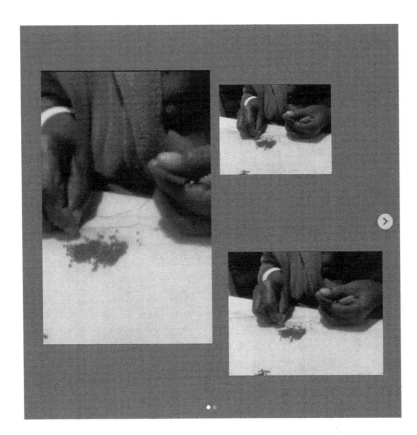

Figure 2.4 The Herd Instagram post, hand work stitching together past and present. © The Herd, reproduced with kind permission of Mbali Mthethwa.

and towards which she feels a sense of respect and responsibility), to reinvigorate it in a way that appeals to a broader base of consumers. While customers who identity with Nguni heritage may feel a special affinity towards The Herd necklaces, people from other cultural backgrounds are also able to appreciate the innovative style and aesthetic offered by the necklaces, and buy one.

The luxury items discussed here are at once new and old, and pay homage to a recognizable set of aesthetics from pre-colonial times while bringing them freshly into the post-colonial present. As such, they can be theorized as a form of communicative time travel – "interludes" – that stitch together past and present through aesthetic form. They reach back to the past to mobilize the power of authenticity and the right to represent, appreciate and bring it into the present in such a way that makes aspects of those cultures legible to customers on an open market. In this way, they certainly commoditize those cultural resources, but that commoditization is coming from within rather than without. Instead of more economically or socially powerful actors reaching in to take, expropriate, steal, or exploit those cultural resources (the pattern of colonial domination), members of that culture are telling their stories their own way, and joyfully offering up the artefacts that they make in the process for wider consumption on the open market. Authenticity, in other words the right of an artist, maker, or designer to tell and capitalize on their own stories, in this process is key. Who has the right to tell a story, and who does not? When a person with a sense of validity and identification within a culture tells their story in their own way, not only is there an integration of ethic with aesthetic, there is also arguably a new form of soft power at play. I turn to this argument next.

Luxury as Modality for African Soft Power

The notion of soft power (Nye, 1990) is usually applied to super-powers, such as the United States or China, who seek to exert influence and produce positive affect for their states through the dissemination of, among other things, creative and cultural goods. It is defined as "the ability to obtain preferred outcomes through attraction" (Nye, 2009: 160), through offering up cultural resources for admiration and enjoyment, rather than a display of dominance. Fashion and design are key modalities of soft power (Frans and Aryani, 2020; Godart, 2014; Thussu, 2016: 29). Although not normally associated with African states (who are normally considered by political theorists to be the recipients of soft power, especially in the case of China's efforts to economically dominate the continent), the possibility of African soft power is associated with the "Africa rising" discourse (Sidiropoulos, 2014: 197). For example, South African fashion designers have been tipped as socio-cultural change agents in the post-apartheid era (Farber, 2010: 128): "These designers and their garments gesture toward […] an 'Afropolitan' aesthetic, in which both African and cosmopolitan aesthetics are reworked and integrated" (Farber, 2010: 129). The celebration of African aesthetics and their presentation to a global marketplace by designers who lay claim to the cultural inheritance of those aesthetics is most certainly an important form of offering up values and aesthetics as a force for attraction, indeed affiliation, with African cultures and the states to which they belong.

African luxury branding functions as a form of soft power in that it captures the communicative influence of African brands that present their values and aesthetics as materials to be appreciated by consumers around the world, thereby deploying the power of attraction. As a form of "moral authority" (Sidiropoulos, 2014), luxury design that is rooted in authentic cultural heritage arguably has a special influence in the global consumer marketplace. As the discussion of Thebe Magugu and The Herd shows, one key branding strategy of African luxury brands is the mobilization of cultural aesthetic resources, narrated as being lovingly and respectfully recovered from the past and re-centred into a newly modernized aesthetic (as opposed to culturally appropriated as would be the case if an outsider, especially a western brand, was to steal the look). This ties in to a shift in narrative that has been opening up globally, partly driven by high profile and aesthetically powerful players such as fashion designers who vocally demonstrate love for and pride in their own cultures. This communicative work actively lifts up African aesthetics and narratives as counter to the denigrating attitudes and appropriating strategies coming from outside. African entrepreneurs and consumers are less and less willing to accept attitudes that suggest that their cultures and aesthetics are in some way inferior, and are actively doing the work required to create strong messages in the public realm that counter the racist stereotypes so often attached thereto. As this chapter has shown, luxury brands are an important part of this sea-shift in communication about African aesthetics. Because of their global aspirations and the attention achieved from around the world, their brands play a special role in re-writing the script of what "African" means in the global consumer marketplace, and introducing authentic narratives of heritage, beauty, and connection to the past.

As argued in the context of Chinese luxury brands, "a heritage brand captures aspects of [...] history to be communicated as an authentic foundation for brand identity and communications" (Schroeder et al., 2017: 6). From this perspective, it can be argued that Thebe Magugu and The Herd are deploying cultural authenticity in order to position their brands as luxury, and their commodities as linked directly to artisanal skill and indigenous meanings. Both brands walk the line of carefully and cleverly balancing out the presentation of cultural heritage with broader market and design appeal. If the items were "too" Sotho or Zulu, some potential customers might be alienated or feel that they don't have the right to appreciate or wear such items, for fear of cultural appropriation. But if the items are not Sotho or Zulu "enough," they lose their unique originality, and the special aesthetic sensibility that makes them attractive and interesting. While some African customers are excitedly searching out luxury items that speak to and represent their sense of self, including their rich cultural heritages, other customers are seeking items that square with a more generic sense of style and design excellence, which both Thebe Magugu and The Herd achieve. The success of African luxury brands that successfully "sell" some version of cultural heritage is that they do so elegantly, explicitly yet subtly, in objects that can be considered objectively beautiful. They are not directly commoditizing cultural resources, they are re-making them into original goods that retain a strong narrative of inspiration and affiliation with those resources.

Consuming Africa? Afropolitanism and Commodification

It is important not to overstate the potency of African luxury as soft power. While the presence of African brands in important cultural products such as huge blockbuster Hollywood films, or being worn by stars like Beyoncé, certainly adds to the affective pull and moral value of a generalized sensibility of Africanness, the global luxury industry does not represent a level playing field in which African brands centring heritage and cultural authenticity are able to compete on equal terms. Many of the African luxury brands that have emerged in the past decade, despite being incredibly innovative and matching their international peers in terms of creativity and vision, have to operate in the context of the precarious infrastructures, gross inequality, and poor governance that characterize many African economies, South Africa included. Although they succeed in creating magnificent products that meet luxury standards, there is no doubt that business potential can be hampered by limiting regulatory environments, high tax, corruption, or even plain incompetence.

It is important to critically assess the extent to which the specifics of Sotho or Zulu culture, to stay with the case studies examined in this chapter, are received as such by global markets, or if they continue to homogenize the diversity of cultures present on the continent into a mash-up, sanitized, and commoditized version of Africanness that some critique as "Afropolitanism" (Dabiri, 2016). Although the specifics of particular spiritual and cultural belief systems are integrated in authentic ways into, say a poncho or necklace, they may well be read by the global audience as African rather than Basotho or Nguni. And despite the power of African designers using luxury as a modality to speak for themselves and represent their own cultures with pride and artfulness to the world, thereby "redressing the balance," there remains a problem in that "we still do not hear the narratives of Africans who are not privileged" (Dabiri, 2016: 105). Although Mbali Mthethwa and Thebe Magugu come from disadvantaged backgrounds, they have both achieved a level of fame and recognition for their creative talents. As such they have entered an elite sector of the creative industry in which they are respected as businesspeople and admired as trend-setters. Further, as the author Yewande Omotso points out in an interview, "the term Afropolitan only seems useful for the West as it gives the West an opportunity to understand and even 'consume' Africa" (Fasselt, 2015: 235).

This critique is important: it highlights the question of whether, even in authentic luxury brand narratives that celebrate a unique aspect of an African culture in such a way as to pay homage through a sense of inheritance and ownership rather than appropriation, the translation of that heritage into a commodity strips away that claim to authenticity. In other words, does the commodification of the cultural heritage item – the blanket, the beads – cancel out the authentic celebration of that heritage, in that it is simply being packaged (albeit in a beautiful and ethical way) for the consuming gaze of the outsider? Indeed, the "Africa Rising" narrative can and should be critiqued: "it is just that, a story, where growth-for-growth's sake replaces development and the agenda of industrialization and moving Africa up the global production chain has been discarded" (Taylor, 2014: 22). The growing visibility of African luxury brands, and the nuggets of cultural heritage that they celebrate, although certainly producing important economic activity in the creative and cultural industries, is not enough to reverse the centuries of exploitation, structural adjustment and marginalization that African economies have suffered. Is luxury centred on cultural heritage a mere red herring then, for the challenges facing African economies? Can luxury contribute to lessening inequality and improving the quality of life for more Africans, or does it instead exploit that inequality, and merely package Africanness into newly glamorous and desirably bite-sized chunks to be consumed at will by fashionistas around the world?

One of my interview participants, Lindiwe, an entrepreneur based in South Africa, has thought a lot about the kind of support that the luxury sector needs from government. She thinks that not enough is being done "to try and help the industry grow." She argues that luxury start-ups need state support in order to not remain start-ups, to be able to grow from being the "designer at the corner store" into globally recognized brands. What is at play here is a whole-hearted acceptance of the neo-liberal logic of limitless growth. Luxury businesses are expected to aim for nothing less than global recognition, and for brands to go global is seen as the ultimate business success. Entrepreneurs are expected to want more than the "corner shop" from which to sell their wares, and to be driven by an ambition of global fame and fortune. This viewpoint was shared by many of the luxury entrepreneurs I interviewed. The idea of international recognition and reaching global markets was repeatedly used as an indicator of success. In the context of existing non-African luxury brands, which are desired and acquired by consumers all over the world, the precedent for achievement has clearly been set. African luxury brands aim to go global, and many of them are succeeding in that project by using their cultural resources in order to offer an authentic contribution to the global creative economy.

However, it is important to note that the notion of essential, authentic Africanness is in itself unstable. Although Basotho blankets have a special connection to Basotho culture, they are actually items with a more complex provenance. Of the two companies that produce them, one is based in Britain and the other in South Africa, owned by Italian immigrants who came to the country after World War 2 (https://www.aranda.co.za/pages/about). The blankets feature specially Sotho motifs, but also symbols that signal a British influence, for example crowns and playing cards. These features make them no less Basotho; the point here is that every culture and aesthetic practice is forged and produced through a variety of resources, and the Basotho blanket is no different. Similarly, the Nguni beaded necklaces are made from "Japanese seed beads" and "Miyuki beads" (@the-herdsa Instagram post, 24 January 2019). Again, this does not make the necklaces less Zulu, but shows how Zuluness has every right to integrate resources from elsewhere in its aesthetic self-construction and expression. In short, clinging too tightly to an essentialist notion of African culture is problematic, because all cultures are dynamic, multi-faceted, eclectic, porous, and draw on others in complex ways. African luxury brands are drawing on complex histories of international trade, exchange and innovation, while participating in those same webs in new ways in the present. It is impossible for creative work to trade outside of capitalism, and although there is certainly an argument that could be made about the perils of the commodification of culture, if anyone has a right to commodify a culture it is the person who was born into it, and suffered its marginalization by others.

3 Back to Nature: Beauty and African Luxury Minimalism

This chapter explores African luxury brands that favour a minimalist aesthetic and ethic. To give some context for the theme of African luxury minimalism, first I present some important comments from interview participants, who had strong feelings about excess in African creative industries. Then, I present two Black-woman owned brands that use minimalism in important ways aesthetically: the first is a nude-tone underwear brand designed for African skin hues, Gugu Intimates, the second is an all-natural skin and hair care brand, also designed for African skin and hair textures, Suki Suki Naturals. After showing how these brands deploy minimalism in unique ways that also point towards a more complex set of ethical issues and questions, I bring the case studies together theoretically in the final section of the chapter with the help of Black feminist theories. While the brands use minimalism both in the creation of their luxury commodities and their communication, these are both linked in important ways to what I call a "botanical ethic," which offers a new orientation towards decolonial relations with the land, and the emancipatory politics of Black feminist thought.

Against Excess: African Designer Views on Minimalism

There is a stereotype of African aesthetics as "extra" – highly colourful, bold and bright, in general outside or beyond some sense of normal, or "big" (as style and narrative in the *Coming to America* films handily summarize). For example, Simidele Dosekun has written at length about the politics, both personal and trans-national, of the hyper-feminine stylings of some women in Lagos, who wear the highest of heels, the shortest of miniskirts, the longest false nails and lashes, and most elaborate weaves (Dosekun, 2020). This look relates to the "bling" aesthetic favoured by many pop stars and rappers famous in African and African-American popular cultures. The stereotype here is that

DOI: 10.4324/9781003227038-3

African wealth, especially when associated with women, is expressed in the vivacious and conspicuous consumption of luxury items, which are boldly and happily displayed on both body and social media sharing. Such an attitude is reinforced by academic writings on "conspicuous" consumption in Africa (Posel and Van Wyk, 2019).

In contrast to this "extra" aesthetic, some African luxury brands intentionally champion minimalism as the key aesthetic to their design sensibility and communications. This demands critical analysis. What does it mean, when consumer brands construct a quiet, understated look and feel, that emphasizes "natural" forms and substances, and simple, elegant aesthetics, yet nevertheless position these as deeply luxurious *and* authentically African?

Esmé, a fashion designer based in Accra, took pains to explain that to her, luxury was mostly about simplicity and quality. Luxury, she argues, should not be complicated, but "straight to the point" rather than "trying to do anything avant-garde." She wants her customers to "get value" from her clothes rather than to be overwhelmed with fussy, intricate details. One of her signature styles is a range of crisp, architectural white shirts, which she describes as "versatile, no fuss." She explains, "we're not trying to give you some out-of-the-moon experience, we're just doing [shirts] better, that's all." The ethic here is that simplicity itself is the ultimate luxury. Rather than dressing her shirts up with complicated embellishments, Esmé creates them to be extremely minimalist in colour, texture, and silhouette, and that is where her design ethic lies. Esmé feels so strongly about her "straight to the point" ethic that she refuses even to name her label "luxury." Her rationale is that, especially in the context of African cities where sub-standard products are flagrantly labelled luxurious, that luxury should *speak for itself*. She elaborates, "If you're given a service or a product and its luxurious, you don't even open your mouth to say it's luxurious. Do I need to tell people I'm trustworthy, I'm honest?" Esmé's rhetorical questions indicate that luxury should speak for itself, rather than have to name itself. She knows her simple garments are deeply luxurious, and trusts that her customers can see it. The implication is that true luxury can be achieved through simplicity, quality design, and crafting, rather than excessive embellishment. In all her brand communications, Esmé reinforces this insistence on a commitment to "minimalism" rather than excess. This squares with research that has found that sometimes, "'less' is more effective than 'excessive' in signalling wealth" (Liu et al., 2018).

Saachi is Esmé's contemporary, also a fashion designer, based on the other side of the continent in Nairobi. She argues that this idea that "the more you have the wealthier you are" is a western import. In

Africa, she concludes, "we don't need that, we are minimalist." Saachi sees her brand – which features hand-embroidered pieces and limited-edition ranges of silk dresses and jackets – as part of a movement in the moral education of African consumers, where excess in terms of quantity is replaced by minimalism in terms of quality.

> We need to create awareness, starting with the middle class, that we don't need to go buy our kids ten pairs of jogging pants, instead we should get one of the best quality, so you can pass it down and around.

She argues that in Africa, well-paid jobs are the true luxury, and she wants her brand to be part of a move towards sustainable high-end fashion that invests in local communities and skills rather than fast fashion, and where middle- and upper-class consumers choose "small but useful wardrobes" over throwing away dozens of black bags of H&M clothes every year, like they do in America. Although some of Saachi's designs are quite colourful and embellished, her collections nonetheless are quite minimalist in terms of the quantity of items produced, and her choice of natural and sustainably sourced fabrics, like locally woven silk.

Both Esmé and Saachi are presenting a version of minimalism as central to their thinking and business practice about what luxury fashion means in African contexts. Esmé speaks from the aesthetic position, and argues that design should be straight to the point rather than fussy and complicated, while Saachi speaks to the importance of buying fewer, better quality items, that is, the ethics of consumption in Africa. Both these ethical positions in relation to minimalism also play a role in some key branding discourses that I have observed in other luxury brands working on the continent. Taking this as a starting point, I explore how minimalism shows up in African luxury branding. I do this through a close look at two chosen case studies, both companies started and owned by Black women and offering luxury products to Black women consumers, which build strongly on notions of simplicity and a "back to basics" rationale.

Self-Care and Luxury: With Nude and Nature

To further explore the complex meanings of minimalism, and how it is deployed in unique ways in the discourses of African luxury brands, I take a focus on brands that focus on body care. While fashion clothing enrobes and adorns the body and is often the site of elaborate and bold aesthetic work, personal items for body, skin, and hair, are connected more directly with the politics of self-care, embodied as it is. Self-care is a highly gendered domain, with women most persistently hailed by consumer media and luxury discourses to regimes of self-management and aesthetic labour (Elias et al., 2017). While gender is of course a continuum of performativity, and consumer culture has increasingly been celebrating the arrival and activity of non-binary personae and styles, for example the online movement of men wearing make-up championed by Rihanna's make-up brand, Fenty, there remain certain heteronormative power relationships evident. While many men can go through life never having moisturized their skin, never mind having thought long and hard about which moisturizer is right for their particular skin type, this is a very normal set of ideas and practices for most middle and upper class women. In African consumer cultures, clothing, hair-care, and skin-care are promising new markets for entrepreneurs, because the mainstream (white-owned) political economy of the beauty industry has marginalized and offended Black women. Beauty is therefore a site for politicized aesthetics organized around body positivity and pride. I explore two case studies to take these arguments further.

Skin Tone Politics and Consumer Equality in Gugu Intimates

Founded by Gugu Nkabinde in 2016, Gugu Intimates is an underwear brand that offers Black women a range of skin-tone nude underwear (Labase, 2017). As stated on its website,

> It's hard to imagine that until now, skin colored underwear for brown skinned girls has not been a thing – with all the shades and tones of melanin-rich goddesses walking this African continent. This is why this brand is for US. Brown skinned girls – beautiful in every shade.

The range is simple, but the styling is luxurious in that simplicity. Five shades of brown are named for the words "beauty" in five African languages: Elewa (Yoruba), Buhle (Zulu/Xhosa), Amara (Arabic), Zuri (Swahili), and Runako (Shona). The company offers two styles of bra and two styles of underpants (which retail for just under R1,000 per set, excluding delivery – making it certainly in the luxury price range), and one full-piece swimsuit. The main selling point of the brand is the range of nude shades in which the simple, well-designed underwear items are available. Instead of fussy materials and impractical coverage, as is often present in other luxury brand underwear ranges, Gugu Intimates focuses on fit, comfort and the buttery texture of soft fabrics that provide a "seamless" fit.

The main ethic of the brand is the celebration of the beauty and diversity of skin tones in Black and Brown women. In an industry interview, Nkabinde explains, "It baffled me that on a continent with multiple skin tones when you said 'nude' there was no underwear that matched an African person." (https://www.yoco.com/za/blog/article/gugu-intimates-nude-underwear-for-african-women/). The styling of the brand is minimalist, with a focus on full-length portraits of women wearing the undergarments. In a campaign tagged #TheNewNaked, as shared on Instagram on 13 February 2020, five beautiful women wearing Gugu Intimates bras and briefs pose in a group portrait (see Figure 3.1). They are all healthy and curvaceous, with flat stomachs and smooth, glowing skin. The tones of the women's skin is centre stage, alongside the underwear that matches or complements it so well. The caption emphasizes classic design, and plays on the notion of "basic," arguing that even though the underwear items are exceedingly simple in their design, they exude luxury in their texture, shape, fit, and sensibility. This image is reproduced in various locations across the brand messaging, signalling it's importance in communicating the main narrative the brand seeks to promote. The group portrait beautifully captures the diversity in skin tone and hair style of Black African women – though it does not represent much body diversity. The women used in the campaign have normal bodies: they are not stick-thin models, they have thighs and tummies, and are not overly touched up so as to seem artificial, nevertheless, they are within the range of bodies considered acceptable by consumer culture. This represents the current sizing range available in the brand, which promises on its website that bigger sizes are in development and will become available soon – it is likely that more body positive "fat" models will be included in the campaign at some future time. For now, it is worth focussing on the skin tone politics and aspects of Black pride that are deployed in the campaign. It is significant that Nkabinde obliquely refers to the Blue Ivy/Beyoncé song, "Brown Skin Girl" in her branding. The song celebrates the existence of Black women, and offers a rallying call for self-love and appreciation, and offers adulation for Black, especially dark-skinned, celebrities like Naomi Campbell and Lupita N'yongo, who offer affirmative role models for Black girls:

Pose like a trophy when Naomi walks in
She need an Oscar for that pretty dark skin
Pretty like Lupita when the cameras close in
(Extract from Brown Skin Girl, by Beyoncé).

Figure 3.1 Nothing Basic about Gugu Intimates. Photograph by Jeffrey Rikhotso. © Gugu Intimates, reproduced with kind permission of Gugu Nkabinde.

Referencing the pop song in the brand values demonstrates an explicit connection to the growth in celebration and pride in Black femininity around the world. This is also visually communicated in much of the photography for the #NewNaked campaign, especially the group portrait shown in Figure 3.1. Group portraiture has been used in advertising in order to obliquely reference important works in art history, which gesture to social hierarchies and relationships in visual form (Schroeder, 2008). In this context, the group portrait is used to signal a warm, supportive sense of sisterhood, love, and solidarity among Black women. They stand in an intimate posture: hand on the other's waist or thigh, elbow leaning on the other's shoulder. Of course, the implied intimacy is partly playing off a homoerotic sexiness that most advertising seeks to sell in its imagery and thereby to associate it with the products on offer. That the five women are conventionally beautiful in the way that usually carries consumerism's stamp of approval, and wear only their underwear underlines the postfeminist sensibility (Gill, 2007) of the core brand message: happy and empowered women are sexy, willing to display their bodies, and actualize their empowerment through accessing and displaying luxury commodities of their choosing.

There is an important political ethic that comes through, that cannot be ignored. Gugu Intimates is a brand that is achieving recognition and success in the age of #BlackLivesMatter and #MeToo, where Black people and women are forced to continue to protest their oppression and injury by white supremacy and capitalism (part of the same toxic structure). As such, when a "nothing for us without us" brand is established by a Black woman, which sells items specially designed and manufactured with the interests and pleasure of Black women in mind, it is crucial to fully recognize the political aspects of the brand statements being made. Nkabinde is a Black woman, a marketing expert, and entrepreneur, and has cogently tapped into the rise in an affirmative vocabulary and politics that recognizes and celebrates the diversity of Black skin tones. Celebrities are often at the forefront of the mainstreaming of woke ethics. Beyoncé and other famous African and African-American women make huge contributions to healing historical injuries through creative works that see, recognize, and show love for people who have been oppressed, exploited, and injured by the systems of sexist racial capitalism (hooks, 2007, 2014). This is not to suggest that the creation of new woman-centric and Black-pride aesthetics is enough to right the wrongs of the past, but to recognize the important role that creativity and communication can play in this process. With this in mind, it is useful to put the branding of skin-tone underwear for Black women into dialogue with other forms of visual communication that use the politics of skin tone and consumer exclusion to say something about the operations of racism in South Africa.

Figure 3.2 shows an important artwork by South African artist and critical theorist Thembinkosi Goniwe. The work was part of an exhibition in Cape Town in 2000, *Returning the Gaze*, curated by the Black Artists Collective (BLAC), which "according to its draft proposal for discussion, called upon black cultural workers 'to return the

Figure 3.2 Returning the Gaze, Thembinkosi Goniwe, Billboard, 2002 ©
Thembinkosi Goniwe, reproduced with his kind permission.

gaze, turn the tables of history by creating a platform and structure for
representations of whites by Blacks'" (Sobopha, 2001: 56). Goniwe's
contribution was particularly striking, and all the more powerful in
that it was installed on a billboard on a street near the University of
Cape Town's Lower Campus. It "showed portraits of two men,
Goniwe, and fellow artist and lecturer, Professor Malcolm Payne.
Both had a Bandaid strip on the cheek. A 'flesh coloured' strip"
(Williamson, 2002).

It is significant that the artwork was included as a public intervention in the city of Cape Town, which is well known for its highly
problematic racist exclusion of Black customers especially from its
service industry (Ndlovu, 2022). Inserting the "flesh-coloured"
Bandaid into the portraits of the two men immediately revealed the
racism at the heart not only of the plaster strip industry, and all other
associated consumer industries that market things as flesh-tone or
nude, but indeed the whole structure of a consumer and services society that takes its natural customer to be white, and customers of
other skin tones as somehow intervening in the white spaces of consumerism. As has been explored in depth by black feminist theory and
cultural studies (Collins, 2000; Gqola, 2001; hooks, 2007, 2014; Pinto,

2013), Black women have been doubly injured by the systems of racism and sexism. White supremacy mandated blackness as other, but this also translated into forms of colourism within Black communities, where lighter-skinned Black people are often privileged (Hunter, 2002, 2007, 2013). Despite the huge diversity in skin tones in humanity, plaster companies persist in producing just one pale beige version of the item. Artists are usually at the avant-garde of political image-making. In the early 2000s, Goniwe made his very important intervention highlighting the ubiquity of racism in everyday moments of consumption, such as not being able to use a skin-tone plaster for a small graze. These many micro-aggressions add up to a structure of oppression that is overwhelming. It is actually quite surprising that industry didn't pivot more quickly to serving Black and Brown customers. It was only in 2020, after the horrific murder of George Floyd by a white police officer and the upsurging of protest in the form of #BlackLivesMatter in the United States that Bandaid released a range of "racially inclusive adhesive strips" (Klein, 2020). Considering the timing of the release, this could certainly be read as a form of "woke-washing" (Sobande, 2019), in that the brand was trying to capitalize on the upsurge in activism and black pride consciousness in the wake of the ongoing police brutality in the USA. Although Goniwe's piece should not be read as a piece of consumer activism, in that it is saying much more than that plaster companies should diversify their product ranges, in some ways it is prescient of the current moment in which the politics of racism and skin tone is pulled into the consumer spotlight. There is arguably a similar politics at play in the visual interventions of Gugu Intimates, albeit two decades after Goniwe's billboard.

South Africa has changed in the 20 years between Goniwe's important provocation and the emergence of a brand like Gugu Intimates, which seeks to commercialize the political sensibility of equality. Although more unequal than ever – in that the Gini coefficient has changed from 59 in 2000 to 63 in 2020 – there is also a bigger Black South African middle class than ever, and also a significant wealthy Black elite that is highly visible in the media. The politics of gendered racial inclusivity has more currency than ever, and it is significant that a Black woman-owned brand is championing Black skin tone diversity. Luxury brands by definition cannot be democratic and inclusive, as they project an exclusivity and rarity and their products are highly priced. Nkabinde herself notes that her target market is *high-income* black women, because her products are niche due to being expensive to produce (Labase, 2017). I will return to the politics of commoditizing racial inclusivity through luxury later in this chapter. For now, I will address another thematic, looking at the role of essential botanicals in luxury brands tapping into the "self-care" discourse.

Essential Botanicals and Natural Grooming in Suki Suki

Suki Suki is a skin and hair care brand that frames itself as "Uniquely African. Authentically Natural." Founded by Congolese-South African entrepreneur, Linda Gieskes-Mwamba, "who was born in Kinshasa, Democratic Republic of Congo (DRC), but grew up in Brussels and Johannesburg" (https://sukisukinaturals.co.za/about-suki-suki/?v=edb5dc74af1c), the brand prioritizes natural, essential botanicals in manufacture and messaging. With a highly minimalist logo, of the brand name typographically set against a white background, Suki Suki offers a skin care range featuring face oils, a face scrub/mask, and a hydrating mist specially formulated for melanin-rich skin, and a hair care range featuring shampoo, conditioner, and moisturizing butters and sprays, formulated for curly and coily hair.

The ethic of non-toxicity is key: the brand claims to offer harm-free beauty products that are specially tailored for African bodies and climates. In counterpoint to consumer industries specially targeting Afro hair and skin, Suki Suki offers all-natural alternatives free from chemicals, parabens, and other harmful substances.

> Our mission is simple: to create natural products that nurture, soothe and heal skin and hair with harm-free ingredients from Mother Nature's pantry. We're passionate about the quality of our ingredients, and focus on unique and relatively undiscovered African specialties like Prickly Pear, and under-utilised natural remedies like Papaya and Mango. Our uniquely formulated and handcrafted recipes celebrate Africa's rich and diverse plant life while keeping you free from harmful and artificial chemicals (https://sukisukinaturals.co.za/about-suki-suki/).

Further, Suki Suki promises its customers, "that our products are free from mineral oil, preservatives, parabens, sulfates, phthalates, formaldehyde, petroleum, paraffin and animal testing." Notably, the move away from toxic cosmetics is framed as luxurious: "We believe that your skin and hair – the body's largest organ and its crown respectively — should be treated with love and the most luxurious ingredients available" (https://sukisukinaturals.co.za/about-suki-suki/).

One of the key ingredients in one of the brand's facial oils is prickly pear, which is presented as a key "miracle" ingredient, alongside others such as papaya, rosehip, shea, and acai. The products are named for their main botanical ingredient, thus spotlighting the essential natural source and offering consumers an opportunity to imagine the plant from which the substance comes that they will be applying to their skin or hair. Figure 3.3 shows an Instagram post featuring a pile of prickly pears on a table in a Moroccan riad. The pears appear to have been just picked off the cacti and imply an organic farm-to-table sensibility. The message being constructed by the image, and its caption, which gestures to the "super" properties of the fruit, is that there is minimal space and time between the harvesting of the fruit and the application of their oil to the skin,

Figure 3.3 An African "superfruit" and "miracle" skin care ingredient. Image © Nomad Marrakech and re-produced with their kind permission.

and that there is a direct material connection between the natural states of the source of the oil and its destination. The image is presenting the "nature" in "natural," offering an illustration of the botanical source of the substance as evidence for it having been harvested from African flora, rather than having been chemically produced in a laboratory, as many cosmetics are. The ethic of extracting essential, natural substances is presented as not only lacking in the kinds of toxins that are central to the lab process, but as a way of connecting with nature in an authentic way.

Black women's skin and hair have been on the receiving end of toxic chemicals for hundreds of years. The skin lightening industry has perniciously profited from racism and colorism, selling toxic chemicals that bleach dark skin (Thomas, 2012, 2020). Similarly, noxious substances in the form of hair relaxers have been marketed as ways to straighten the natural coils and kinks of Black hair, even though these have been shown to have negative long-term consequences for health and happiness (Miranda-Vilela et al., 2014; Shetty et al., 2013). In short, toxicity is an important component of the political economy of the racist standards to which Black women have been subjected for as long as white power has controlled the beauty industry. The market for skin lightening products as well as wigs and weaves, remains significant, and many companies selling such wares try to associate their brands with bling, luxury sensibilities, while remaining vague on the source of ingredients and potential harm they may cause (for example, consider Cameroonian pop star Dencia's range of skin lighteners, Whitenicious). In contrast, Suki Suki prioritizes a calm, understated aesthetic, and an emphasis on the organic origins of its ingredients.

There is an underlying politics to the discourse of "natural" cosmetics, which is significant as a form of ethical consumption linked to holistic wellness and the rejection of the toxic ingredients associated with big pharma. Natural feminine beauty is positioned in opposition to the kind of "fake" beauty of the "hyper-feminine" aesthetic (hair extensions, wigs and weaves, false nails and eyelashes, cosmetic enhancements, and so on). Suki Suki founder, Gieskes-Mwamba, embodies the beauty values offered by the brand: as pictured on the brand website, she possesses smooth, clear, and radiant skin, and a magnificent head of natural hair with perfect kinks and curls. She has an understated yet elegant dress sense and wears little make-up. Although the aesthetic of "natural" feminine beauty is arguably a cross-cultural and cross-racial phenomenon, it takes on special resonance when considering beauty politics in relation to Black women. And, when Black women are the entrepreneurs presenting an alternative set of tools to the market, for beautification and care of the body, skin, and hair, the significance of a "natural" approach takes on an important ethical dimension. If mass-produced, laboratory-manufactured cosmetics that injure both physical well-being and self-esteem are products of white colonial capitalism, then surely sourced-from-nature, non-toxic, and small-batch cosmetics are products of Black commercial and cultural empowerment. Of course this binary is not absolute, but it is joyful to see natural body-care products for and by Black women working in opposition to the white, masculine power of the global pharma-cosmetics industry.

Many Black women still choose weaves and hair straighteners, and indeed there is a precedent in the consumer media industries for predominantly including images of Black women when their presentation comes closer to a "white" aesthetic in terms of body shape and hairstyle (Pilane and Iqani, 2016), which may hint at reasons for the enduring popularity of whitening products. Nevertheless, there is an emerging natural hair movement, in which Black women nurture and celebrate the natural textures, styles, and shapes of African hair as a key aesthetic element of Black feminist politics (Norwood, 2018). Suki Suki positions itself firmly at the heart of the natural hair movement, offering Black women the products needed to transition away from dependency on weaves and chemical relaxers, and to fully embrace their natural hair in stylish ways. As Figure 3.4 shows, the Miraculous Oil is purported to promote hair growth, strengthen and repair, nourish and enhance shine. The product contains "vitamin E-rich Moroccan Argan Oil, Kalahari Melon Seed Oil for moisture, Marula Oil for protection and moisture retention and Baobab Oil for hair growth" (https://sukisukinaturals.co. za/product/miraculous-oil-100ml/). All of these natural sources are notably African, and associated with natural landscapes. In the same way that the pile of prickly pears evokes a desert landscape, these ingredients listed suggest key scenes from the topography and terrain of the continent. The brand imagery deployed by Suki Suki makes explicit links between the botanicals used in the products and the women who will use them. In Figure 3.4, a model is shown applying the Miraculous Oil to her hairline, at the parting in her voluptuous afro. The image is close-cropped, suggesting intimacy, which is further underlined by her bare arms and shoulders.

Self-care is a key discourse in Black feminist thought (Dale et al., 2018; Scott, 2017). As summarized by the oft-invoked provocation from Audre Lorde (Byrd et al., 2009), in the context of the systematic removal of opportunities for joy and happiness for Black women by white supremacist patriarchy, any form of self-care is a revolutionary

Figure 3.4 Suki Suki's "miraculous oil" is specially formulated for natural African hair. Image © Suki Suki Naturals, and re-produced here with kind permission.

act. In consumer culture we see the rise of beauty practices directed at Black women that are packaged in the language of self-care. This is not to suggest that the political content of self-care is evacuated by consumerist aspects, but to shine a light on the nuances and complexities inherent in the many ways in which self-care is actualized in both commercial and personal politics. Personal well-being became "an ideology" in the late 20th century (Erfurt-Cooper, 2009), in that neoliberalism placed an expectation on people that they become individually responsible for their well-being, and should invest in it through market exchange. Feminist critique has highlighted how the injunctions of neo-liberalism to self-management fall more heavily on women and feminine people, who are expected to constantly produce and reproduce a sanitized and attractive appearance in order to be considered worthy of attention or success.

This post-feminist sensibility (Gill, 2007) is especially pernicious in consumer culture, where women have internalized the idea that in order to be free and feel empowered, they have to present themselves and their bodies as sexy, slender, well-styled, and smooth: in short, they must act like good consumers to be seen as "good" women. A large part of these injunctions relate to body work: hair removal, hair styling, skin care, gym, botox, cosmetic procedures, the list is almost endless (Elias et al., 2017). How does the natural skin and hair care movement relate to this constant aesthetic labour that women are expected to perform? On the one hand, we might decry the ongoing injunctions to conform to a consumerist ideal, now presented in the form of Black feminine pride. On the other hand, it is worth considering the extent to which "natural" beauty care regimes are less onerous, healthier, and might in fact free up time, as well as encourage a connection to a sense of fulfilment and pride about the way one's body or skin looks and feels in its natural state. Hair care (and by extension other forms of embodied self-care) can contribute to mental health and well-being: "healing modalities in traditional African societies reveals the influential role of hair and spirituality in holistic wellness practices" (Mbilishaka, 2018: 382).

Beauty Minimalism and Black Feminist Subjectivities

Thus far, this chapter has shown how minimalism manifests in two ways in African luxury branding. The first is through a political reclaiming of the concept of "nude" by Gugu Intimates, the second is through the understated celebration of the concept of "natural" by Suki Suki. As should be evident by now, both brand messages are embedded in key ideas associated with Black femininity: the politics of skin tone, and natural beauty aesthetics. I now turn to exploring the ways in which African luxury minimalism intersects with structures of power, specifically in relation to race and gender. Nudity and nature are two ideas that have historically been associated with Black women in racist and sexist ways, so it stands to reason that they too are concepts that can be reclaimed, indeed have been, as a political and aesthetic project by Black women in service to the cause of their own emancipation.

In artist Tracey Rose's 2001 self-portrait (one of a series in which she performs versions of different feminine archetypes), she presents herself as the so-called Venus Hottentot, Sarah Baartman, who in the early 19th century was trafficked from South Africa to Europe as a curiosity to entertain the European public, her naked body humiliatingly put on display (Catanese, 2010; Levin, 2015). Rose draws a direct connection between her own body and Baartman's, but places her re-enactment in the natural world rather than the cities where Baartman was brutalized. The image,

> poses Rose as Eve archetype, nude in a grassy knoll, poised as if startled to attention by a predator. Caught in the moment of pre-capture, her body is robust and she seems unaffected by her own nudity in the exposed setting.
>
> (Murray, 2002: 88)

Rose's vision of Baartman imagines a pre-colonial idyll, where Black women were not yet named "Black" or "women" by racist patriarchy, and they were at peace, in harmony with nature and their own bodies' places therein, at ease in their own skin and neither molesting, nor being bothered by, other life on Earth. Rose's artwork explicitly locates Black femininity corporeally within natural landscapes. This artwork poignantly gestures towards the sensibilities of both "nude" and "nature," which have been reclaimed and re-deployed by Black women in branding projects for their entrepreneurial concerns, as this chapter has shown. I argue that a similar set of values to those captured in Rose's Venus Baartman – at once emancipatory and nostalgic, and deeply connected to Black feminist theories – are at play in the branding strategies used by Gugu Intimates and Suki Suki Naturals. The remainder of this chapter elaborates on this argument.

Mother Nature: Gender and Botanica! Messaging

Pumla Dineo Gqola, in a seminal discussion on representations of Sarah Baartman, reminds us that colonial power put Black people, women especially, in the same category as animals, characterizing and treating them similarly (Gqola, 2010: 63). Indeed, a significant trope in the colonial imaginary was of an unpeopled, pristine African landscape that was open for occupation, hunting, and extraction, and where the people already living on the land were grouped with the fauna, and as such considered fair targets for violent eradication or enslavement. Perhaps precisely because Europeans imprisoned and enslaved Baartman in the cities of the metropole, many African feminist writers have emphasized the natural landscapes of her home, which they imagine she yearned for, and to which her remains were eventually returned in 2002. Discussing Diana Ferrus' poem, *A Tribute to Sarah Baartman*, which emphasizes imagery of South African landscapes and botanicals, Gqola notes that "home" – framed in the poem as a veld redolent with buchu, mint, and proteas – "is a site of pleasure and ease" (Gqola, 2010: 86). The beautiful landscape from which Baartman was forcibly exiled is visually depicted in Rose's self-portrait, in the poem it becomes a place with "healing possibilities" (Gqola, 2010: 87). Although the stance of Rose-posing-as-Baartman in the self-portrait evokes a sense of imminent threat, an alertness to being hunted perhaps, the verdant field in which she stands seems to hold her, the grasses waving in the wind appear to caress her legs. Her nudity signals her ease with nature, and pride in her body rather than the pain caused by the brutal actions and gazes of white Europeans.

When Black women creatives challenge the stereotypes that have been forced on them, one strategy is to "imagine a world with a sky, a sea, and waves which reflect African women's bodies as a norm rather than a pathology," in other words against the racist, sexist framing of them as "excessively corporeal" (Gqola, 2010: 66). Colonialism sought to empty African landscapes of their indigenous occupants, but when Black women critically or joyfully reinsert themselves in the landscapes of home, they (re-)claim the land as their own. This is something that many white creatives and writers, especially white South Africans, do with ease: claim a form of belonging to the land they conquered. Gqola points out that a claim to belonging, especially to pastoral farmlands, is a key theme in Afrikaans literature, but notes that few Black African writers do the same. Reading this as a consequence of having been violently displaced from the land (Gqola, 2010: 88), her analysis opens up the question of what it means when Black women creatives – be they the writers of literary fiction or the creators of commercial brand messaging – explore a return to the land in their work. In the messaging of Suki Suki Naturals, we can observe a celebration of the organic and the botanical. A strong association is made between the body and the plants that nourish it. Suki Suki stands in for the artful forager, who has the wisdom to differentiate between the many plants in their natural environment, and masterfully select those that are helpful and nourishing, harvesting, and hand-processing so that they can become food, if not for the stomach, for the skin and hair.

This is in contrast to the ways in which the white-owned luxury beauty industry employs a "'safari aesthetic' – a vision of Africa that relies on empty lands, natural assets and tribal culture – to sell pseudo-indigenous luxury to wealthy consumers" (Falkof, 2022: 1). In the brands discussed in this chapter, we see that the narrative of African nature is anthropomorphized, indeed feminized. This speaks to the intersection of feminist and environmental concerns, but it also underlines how femininity is framed as closer to the natural world than masculinity, by western culture at least (which was forcibly imposed on other cultures through colonialism). When Black women position themselves as knowledge producers, and use aesthetic resources of their choosing in that project, a turn to Nature offers a route for excavating pre-colonial structures of knowledge and power, a possible way out of the "safari aesthetic." "Mother Nature" is characterized in popular culture both as wounded, suffering, and neglected, and as a primordial store of a mythical connection to the Earth and its resources, both scientifically known and still mysterious (Roach, 2002). Without falling prey to another form of stereotyping, in which Black African women are pigeon-holed into only one possible identity, for example, as primitively close to nature (another colonial trope), it is worth considering the extent to which Black women have a special right to utilize African botanical resources in their chosen practices of cultural production.

Botanical extraction formed part of the colonial project (Tigner, 2008) and big pharmaceutical companies remain willing to exploit wisdom and knowledge from indigenous peoples around the world. In South Africa, for example, Khoisan knowledge about Hoodia, an indigenous succulent that is known to suppress hunger amongst other uses, has been redeployed into a diet-aid in the West, and not necessarily in ways that the Khoisan community has been able to benefit and profit from, though there is that potential (Foster, 2017). But, when a Black-woman owned brand offers substances like prickly pear oil, baobab oil and Kalahari melon for the use and benefit of (mainly, but certainly not exclusively) Black women customers, a different dynamic is at play. Although of course there remain some forms of extraction and commodification, in African luxury brands using African botanicals, this happens in the modality of "for us by us." This stands in direct opposition to the colonial mentality and process of "stolen from them for use by us": stealing knowledge from the Other, by force and through violent methods, for the profit of white Europeans, and to the detriment of those from whom the resources were taken. Botanical resources extracted from African landscapes should, arguably, be primarily used for the benefit of those who call those landscapes home. Integrating both botanical knowledge and cultural affiliations, Suki Suki presents its natural ingredients as an original source of wellness, offering a direct emotional and aesthetic connection for Black women consumers with "Mother Nature." This branding exercise draws on and rewrites the stereotyping notion of the "safari aesthetic," which is often deployed by the luxury industry to invoke a sense of untamed African wilderness as a resource for touristic pampering.

Connecting back to nature in ways that are framed as empowering to racial and gendered subjectivities is an important ethic and aesthetic in African luxury minimalism. There is resonance of a celebration of environmental resources and an affiliation to the land and all it symbolizes. "The Land" is a highly politicized resource, that links to decolonial demands (Walker et al., 2010). As such, nature-centric luxury brands offer a new narrative about what African aesthetics can and do look like, and could optimistically be read as contributing to the decolonial project, in which Black African people, and women in particular, reclaim their power on both economic and artistic levels.

Power Dialectics in the Branding of Self-Love

There is a striking similarity in the aesthetics offered by Gugu Intimates, in its portraits of magnificent Black women joyfully wearing "nude" and "seamless" underwear matching their diverse brown skins, the intimate close up photographs of beautiful Black women nourishing their hair and skin by Suki Suki Naturals, and Tracey Rose's *Venus Baartman*. In all these images, the bodies, skin and hair of Black women are centre stage, but offered as a normal and natural part of existence rather than made hyper-visible and sexualized by the white and/or male gaze.

Nudity can be read as an act of reclamation, a joyful expression of self-worth and love of the bodies that we have been born with, rather than an objectification of them imposed from the outside, where women are forced to be "naked so that those interested can gawk" (Gqola, 2010: 63). For Black feminists, significant intellectual, emotional, and aesthetic resources are devoted to the project of reclaiming humanity, and restoring dignity to Black women, in short, learning or choosing to love the bodies that have been subjected to so much cruelty for casual enjoyment of others. Gqola analyses a poem by Grace Nichols, in which the "speaking subject lies in her bath, thinking about a world that reflects her interestingly rather than oppressively" (Gqola, 2010: 97). The milieu of bath-time in this piece is significant, because it signals "the possibility of enjoying her own body" (Gqola, 2010: 97), she "appears as self-loving" (Gqola, 2010: 101). The joys of bathroom rituals are celebrated by Suki Suki imagery, in which Black

women are shown enjoying their grooming routines, and are implied in
Gugu Intimates imagery, showing women in their underwear pre-
sumably just before or after ablutions in the privacy of their homes or
their lover's. In the intimacy of private moments and personal acts –
washing one's hair, oiling one's skin, luxuriating in a bath, wandering
around the house in undies – we see a quiet celebration of existence,
and the right to happiness embodied in physical, material ways.

African luxury minimalism, as manifested by the brand communications analysed in this chapter, can be directly linked with the
emancipatory politics of self-representation. Although the images
used by both Gugu Intimates and Suki Suki naturals are portraits in
the tradition of advertising and magazine cover photography – including professional lighting, styling, studio settings, and careful
post-production strategies – they can also be linked with rise of self-
portraiture in popular culture. A growing body of scholarship has
examined the aesthetics and politics of selfies (Frosh, 2015; Iqani and
Schroeder, 2016), and many agree that this increasingly prevalent
genre of image is central to the politics of expression and emancipation (Abidin, 2016; Kedzior and Allen, 2016; Kuntsman, 2017):
the claiming of space and demands for the right to exist and be seen
on terms defined by the makers and subjects of the images. In the
spirit of "nothing for us without us," the body positivity movement
uses portraiture and self-portraiture to claim space for bodies and
personal aesthetics that have been marginalized or denigrated by
mainstream consumer culture. This space has until recently been
controlled by white supremacist patriarchal power, and this is only
changing due to aesthetic activism to demand a place at the table.
When Black women take charge of the representation of Black
women – as we have seen to be a key communicative strategy in the
African luxury brands discussed in this chapter – a new politics of
representation comes into play. This politics claims the right to represent as one that also narrates joyful, empowering, and meaningful
subject positions.

In luxury products created and marketed by Black women entrepreneurs, we see a specific version of the self-care ethic take shape. It
is productive to consider branding as a site of cultural and creative
expression. Although of course it is tightly tied to the neoliberal project and processes of market exchange, and as such can never be
analysed outside of a critique of capitalism, the creative energies ex-
pended by entrepreneurs, and communications experts in the creation
of luxury products deserves to be taken seriously. "Creative texts offer
an ability to theorize and imagine spaces of freedom unavailable" in

other genres (Gqola, 2010: 71). In African luxury brands created and owned by Black women that create products specially for Black women, an important process of imagining freedom is underway.

Although it is important to acknowledge the emancipatory potential of the communication strategies and representational politics of Black women-owned, African luxury brands selling corporeal products, it is equally crucial that we put these into the context of the power structures of late capitalism. Of the African luxury brands discussed in this chapter, the critique could also be made that a certain problematic trope is being re-emphasized, albeit by the subjects of the images themselves: corporeality is emphasized as a (even *the*) dominant way for African women to enter the public domain (Gqola, 2010: 68). In the case studies looked at in this chapter, Black African women's bodies are entering the public domain purportedly on their terms, yet the traces of embodied commodification remain apparent. Although it may well be difficult to sell products designed to adorn or nourish Black women's bodies without depicting said bodies, could it be said to represent a failure of imagination on the parts of the creatives behind the brands, that they were not quite able to forge communicative forms outside of the proverbial box to which Black femininity has historically been consigned? The use of nature and botanical resources (as discussed in the previous section) is certainly one way of escaping this bind or at least complicating it, but it is notable that representations of the body remain central (albeit often implied) even to brand imagery that relies on tropes of nature. Black women are now themselves using their own bodies as symbols of freedom, yet the question must still be asked, "what happens when the most famously embodied Black subject is imagined creatively in ways that do not foreground her corporeality?" (Gqola, 2010: 69).

The question of whether feminine subjects can be considered empowered merely due their self-presentation as such, is the topic of much debate in feminist theory as well as critical consumer culture studies (Dosekun, 2020; Gill, 2007; Iqani, 2018). This debate is often framed in binary terms: are Black women *empowered* by their self-representations in consumer culture, or are they *exploited* by a capitalist patriarchal structure that has forced them to internalize the practices of their own oppression to the extent that they believe they have chosen it? I argue that it is more productive to take a dialectical approach, which recognizes that all contemporary subjects live within various states of "conditional freedom" (Chouliaraki, 2008: 833). This recognizes the power of the structures within which we live (in short, capitalism and market exchange, without some form of participation in which almost every human being on the planet would not be able to function), but also the individual agency that is an inherent and inherited feature of the experience of being alive (that we can always, to some extent or another exercise choice, even if it is only over the attitude that we take to things externally imposed upon us). Structure and agency, manipulation, and empowerment, are not present in equal measure for everyone. Some individuals and groups suffer more oppression despite successful self-expression, therefore historical and contemporary arrangements of access to power need to be taken into account. Every case study needs to be considered in its own right, in order to identify and analyse the complex mix of control and freedom in operation. In the context of the minimalist African luxury brands explored and theorized in this chapter, the emancipatory work of the Black women owned brands needs to be read in the context of histories of exclusion and brutalization. It would be churlish to minimize the importance of the re-claiming of ownership of the right to find joy in corporeal forms of creative expression, in favour of a critique that reinscribes body politics as a limiting modality. There is arguably more promise and pleasure, in the current moment, to recognize even commercial forms of communication that respect and recognize that right to joy, as making important political contributions to a project of healing and emancipation.

4 Shiny Futures and Afro-Fabulous Queer Luxury

This chapter explores avant-garde image-making from African luxury brands that at once reinforces, defies, and transcends the framings of culture and nature that have been presented and theorized in Chapters 2 and 3. A range of thrillingly original aesthetic messages, styles, and forms, which go well beyond the framings of the joyful presentation of cultural heritage, and the claim to a minimalist connection to nature, are being produced by African luxury brands at the time of writing and researching this book (2017–2022). It is no coincidence that many of these forward-looking aesthetics are linked to, or rooted in, queer culture. This chapter shows how urban and futuristic luxurious modalities are both used by and forged from queer subjectivities, which have been mobilized to create effective brand messaging and have become brands in their own right.

Existing in Style: "People want to shine"

Although smooth, glossy modalities are understood to play an important part in the marketing and promotion of all commodities (Iqani, 2012a, 2012b), this is particularly the case when it comes to luxury items (Thrift, 2008). One of my interview participants, Rebecca, is a well-known fashionista and businesswoman who created a powerful personal brand through savvy Instagram self-promotion. This she then translated into a number of offline business opportunities, including a bricks and mortar designer fashion store in a high end mall, a travel concierge service, and a business consultancy. She explains that social media are powerful because:

> People want more, people want to shine. People want to have money. Social media is the place that people want to shine. People

DOI: 10.4324/9781003227038-4

want nice hair and expensive clothes and to travel business class and to eat in nice restaurants and go to luxury destinations.

(Rebecca)

Rebecca's use of social media to establish her personal brand and business interests means that she knows precisely how, as she puts it, the "gloss of social media drives luxury business." She explains that "To shine means to be seen. To be seen to have everything you want. This will drive the luxury consumer market." In the context of high-end and desirable lifestyles, *shine* summarizes both states of wanting and having, which co-determine one another, in a non-linear fashion. It is not simply that one wants a thing, aspires to have it, acquires it, then the wanting is complete. There is a constant, overlapping cycle of wants and desires in relation to luxury lifestyles, that keep feeding into one another and producing new wants and desires. Rebecca perceives, and indeed has proved it through the establishment of her own business essentially out of the success of a hashtag she created, that social media are a primary site through which a sense of "gloss" can be produced and shared, and where "shining" can be made to happen, and through which consumer aspirations are seen to be produced and consumed. It is difficult, as a cultural theorist, to put it better than Rebecca did: "People want to shine." The gloss of social media drives luxury business. This is partly because people see others shining, but also partly quite simply because they want to create a sense of "shine" in their personal narratives. But they also want to shine in the sense that they are able to display their material acquisition of key items that are meaningful to them personally and that express their personalities and tastes, and that they know have a certain amount of influence in a broader social sense, in that their communities will respond to them.

Shine has been theorized as a key modality for the expression of Black joy, sociality, public creative expression, and visibility (Thompson, 2015). I have written elsewhere about the importance of glossy modalities – in particular, glitter, shine, and glow – for the visual expression of feminine achievement and empowerment for Black women in the South African context (Iqani, 2022). Rebecca was, as far as I could tell from our interview and her social media presence, speaking from a heteronormative positionality – she is a traditionally feminine woman, who describes her personal style as "elegant and tasteful," and the portraits of herself that she shares on social media underline this aesthetic. The way in which she spoke about "shine" certainly aligns with the kinds of celebrity portraiture in which feminine success is pictured as filled with light and reflected off the smooth surfaces of luxury clothing, pampered skin, and expensive accessories. The politics of patina might have broader application.

I would like to put the notion of "shine" as a material practice of glamour (Thrift, 2008) into dialogue with the politics of queer survival and queer happiness, in African contexts. Glitter has been shown to be an important aspect to queer activism in the West (Coleman, 2020). In pride parades in major cities around the world, lesbian, gay, bisexual, trans, and queer plus folk turn up with glitter, rainbow regalia, and fabulous outfits to celebrate their existence and stake a claim for the value that they add to the cities that they call home, through rituals that are at once consumption oriented and political statements (Kates and Belk, 2001; Matebeni, 2018). High profile queer or allied celebrities likewise present elaborately glossy identities that include elegant clothing, flawless make-up and hair, and sometimes glittery or glossy textures – the extreme case of course is drag queen culture (Brennan and Gudelunas, 2017). Many feminine and queer subjects use the injunction to "shine!" as a vocabulary of support for one another's achievements. It is important to recognize the political aspects of this. In a key collection of essays in which queer African activists express parts of their life stories, Dzoe Ahmad, a trans woman from Zimbabwe, concludes her essay on how she and others like her are worthy of love, by saying: "Let your inner beauty shine out" (Pellot, 2021: 17). From this perspective, "shine" speaks to both the claiming of space in society, and the importance of performing one's self-worth in contexts that actively threaten not only well-being, but survival.

In most African countries, homosexuality is criminalized and queer people are openly discriminated against, with violence condoned by governments and society at large (Matebeni et al., 2018). South Africa has equality on the basis of sexual orientation and gender enshrined as a human right in its constitution, although this does not translate into equality on the ground, with much violence and persecution still experienced by queer folk (Pellot, 2021). Because homosexuality is still outlawed in most African countries, a wave of migration has taken place to South Africa by queer Africans experiencing or fearing violence, intimidation or imprisonment (Camminga, 2019). In this context, what might it mean to shine, and how do luxury brands and luxurious identities serve as resources for the project of shining? As I show in this chapter, luxury is a key modality and sensibility through which queer achievement and pleasure is expressed in African popular cultures. As Rebecca alerted me to, wanting to shine is a key modality in African consumer cultures. It is not by chance that queer Africans also underline the sensibility of shine as one central to their self-affirmation and activism. One form of shine is normative, and the other is subversive, yet both seem to be expressed through the material modalities of luxury culture. In the discussion that follows, I explore both the normative and subversive possibilities of shine as a communicative – and moral – modality.

Consuming Queerness in (South) Africa

Queer creatives are at the forefront of new aesthetic and popular culture forms in South Africa, especially in the realm of luxury. Despite the reality of hateful crimes against queer and trans people in South Africa, including a spate of horrific murders in the last decade that have gone un-investigated by the police (Factora, 2021), South Africa's constitution promises equality on the basis of gender and sexuality, and as such, the country has become something of a panacea for queer rights on the continent, at least in image if not in practice. It is significant that some key aspects of queer visibility are taking place through self-representation and media coverage organized around the consumption and display of certain luxury objects and styles, and in turn, queer politics are deployed to create brand value. To explore this further, I present two key case studies: the urban style of illustrator and limited-edition sneaker designer, Karabo Poppy, and the modalities of leather in the furniture design of Rich Mnisi. To conclude the chapter, I consider the complexities of the politics of queer activism being mashed up into luxury branding by considering imagery deployed by upcoming pop star, Desire Marea.

Big Dyke Energy in the Big City: Karabo Poppy

Karabo Poppy Moletsane is an award-winning street artist, illustrator and graphic designer, who has become a celebrity on the basis of her unique visual style, but also the shrewdness of her collaborations with big brands, both global and local, and her own online presentation. A self-proclaimed sneakerhead, who has collected sports shoes since she was a child (Cohan, 2021), she is perhaps most famous for her collaborations with Nike, for whom she has designed three ranges of limited-edition Air Force 1 (AF-1) sneakers. Her ranges for the famous sports brand all sell out in record time (this fact is proudly and prominently displayed on her Instagram profile, which boasts that she was also named as one of "Forbes 30 under 30" – the list of young entrepreneurs to watch). Karabo Poppy AF-1's have been worn by stars of the stature of basketball superstar LeBron James, among others.

Born in Vereeniging, an industrial town on the banks of the Vaal River south-east of Johannesburg, Poppy centres the urban in both look and feel of her illustrations and designs, and in the narratives of self that accompany them. Most images that she posts are taken in urban settings, with cityscapes as backdrops.

There is no commodity more luxurious than the absolutely unique, one-of-its-kind, personally customized item, hand-drawn by a famous artist. Depending on the artist, rarity, and the sneaker brand, such pairs might sell for $1,000 (R20,000) and upwards. And for "Sneakerheads" (Choi and Kim, 2019; Matthews et al., 2021) there is no commodity form more luxurious than sneakers – which are collected and traded often at a healthy profit at the niche end of a mass market trade. Although sneakerheads may not explicitly name as luxurious the sneakers that they desire and collect, the element of rarity is key to the collection modality, which may even involve camping out to get the chance to purchase, or reselling rare items at extremely high prices later (Lux and Bug, 2018). Although Moletsane has collaborated with non-luxury brands, for example high street retailers and Coca-Cola, I argue that her work with Nike in particular, in creating a limited-edition, collectible range of AF-1s, is clear evidence of a luxury sensibility in her entrepreneurial design work. Moletsane has created AF-1 limited-edition ranges for Nike, all of which feature her signature illustration style, which uses thick graphic lines, suggesting the aesthetic of having been hand-drawn by marker, and sometimes urban street-art style portraits. In the 1 of 1 pair of high-tops shown in Figure 4.1, we see simple black dashes and zig-zags emblazoned on a pristine white high-top AF-1 sneaker – the classic white on white look of Nike's original design for this shape. In this piece, Moletsane celebrates her favourite sneaker and marker: the two coming together in a luxury product, the only one of its exact kind, aimed at the Karabo Poppy-Nike sneakerhead. Leaving the famous Nike swoosh unmarked, the rest of the sneaker is covered with lines whose intentional placement is belied by a sense of casualness.

Moletsane's aesthetic is somewhat reminiscent of the famous style of Keith Haring (Montez, 2020), who was embedded in the queer scene of New York City in the 1980s and known for strong linework, black and white palettes, and a street art aesthetic. Haring's work was both critically acclaimed and hugely commercially successful. Similarly, Moletsane is a high profile queer creative in Johannesburg, who often uses her platform to speak out, for example against the murder of LGBTQIA+ people, and to mentor younger creatives, and whose work is firmly situated within the commercial. She describes herself as a graphic artist, not a fine artist. Moletsane's personal style, as can be inferred from her enthusiasm for

Figure 4.1 1 of 1 – Karabo Poppy's hand-customized Air Force 1s, as posted
on Instagram. Fair use of publicly posted image.

sneaker culture, is oriented towards the urban. She prefers street-style
branded sportswear. She wears tracksuits, big t-shirts, bomber jackets, and
of course the ever-present pair of sneakers, either her own designs or from
her expansive collection. She favours a heavy chain and chunky watch as
jewellery. She wears her hair in smooth dreadlocks, and her face features
perfect skin and minimalist make-up. In short, she epitomizes a version of
female masculinity (Halberstam, 2018), and to underline this often hash-
tags portraits of herself as #Tomboy, #Androgynous and #Dyke.

In a post from 29 June 2021 (Pride Month), Moletsane is shown wearing
a Rich Mnisi ensemble (see Figure 4.2). An important fashion designer,
also openly queer, Rich Mnisi is a key player in the South African luxury

Figure 4.2 Karabo Poppy x Rich Mnisi – Big Dyke Energy, as posted on Instagram. Fair use of publicly shared image.

market. His branded clothing and vibrant outfits are ever-present in the celebrity social media circuit, and he is known to collaborate with key influencers and other artists, as well as to centre his own face and body in the presentation of his brand (see the following section for more on this designer and his work). In this particular collaboration, Moletsane is shown wearing a bomber jacket from Mnisi's 2021 "Pride" collection. The jacket features a multi-coloured motif, that integrates a deconstructed zebra print in black and white with a similar pattern reproduced in the colours of the gay pride (rainbow) and trans pride (white, pale pink, and pale blue) flags along with brown, green, and purple. The overall effect is the dazzle camouflage used by military ships, but invigorated with colours that signify the spectrum of human sexuality, gender identity, and desire. As such it works to stand out rather than blend in.

Moletsane wears a white t-shirt under the jacket, and a pair of dark blue trousers featuring the capital "R" of the Rich Mnisi logo. Her posture is nonchalant, and she gazes over her left shoulder, her chin tilted up in a defiant expression. The caption advertises that Rich Mnisi will be donating 10% of proceeds from the sale of his Pride range to a "shelter for LGBTQIA+ minority groups during times of crisis" and along with a raised fist emoji and the gay pride flag emoji, announces "BDE – Big Dyke Energy!" This "Big Dyke Energy" riffs off the aphorism of the popular culture joke about "big dick energy" (Abad-Santos and Grady, 2018), but queers it by turning it into a feature of the female masculinity that Moletsane embodies and celebrates in her online identity. Importantly, the BDE embodied in this image is garbed in high-end luxury fashion and linked to urban street culture. It is significant that the image is geo-tagged as "Johannesburg, South Africa." This location tag underlines Moletsane's commitment to the city as her place of work and the context for the street style that she celebrates, both in her personal fashion choices and in the artworks and items that she creates. Although the background to this image suggests sea and sky, usually Moletsane works in urban spaces, and pictures herself in them too. Johannesburg is often called colloquially the "city of gold" (Beavon, 2005): a nod to the mining rush that established the town, but also to contemporary reasons many people migrate there in order to find their fortunes and seek a better life. As the main economic hub in the country, and indeed continent, Johannesburg is the place where many, including queer folk, seek their own opportunities to shine, and build wealth. Moletsane has struck her own version of "gold" in her creative career, linked as it is to fashion, graphic design, the streets, and urban culture of Johannesburg.

The city is highlighted as a space where it is safe be creative, female, and masculine, where one's affiliation to street culture is not only celebratory, but profitable, because an audience and community of like-minded others is available and appreciative of one's work. I will come back to the important links between queer shine and the urban setting later in this chapter. Next, to deepen the discussion of how queer feeling has come into African luxury branding, I explore the modalities of leather sub-cultures as translated into luxury objects in the work of Rich Mnisi.

Leather and the Luxury Object in Rich Mnisi

As indicated in the previous section of this chapter, Rich Mnisi is an important figure in the South African luxury sector (and is incidentally a favourite brand worn by Karabo Poppy). The "About" section of the brand's website proclaims:

> RICH MNISI is a South African based contemporary multi-disciplinary brand founded in 2015 by the Essence Best in Black Fashion Awards' Emerging Designer of the Year for 2019, Forbes 30 under 30 Class of 2019 inductee, Rich Mnisi. Initially, a creative outlet for Mnisi, hoping to unearth Africa's hidden treasures while also being youthful, contemporary, and modern. The brand was born from Mnisi's yearning to connect deeper with his unique culture and heritage and tell a compelling story through his art – a story of a mysterious past, intriguing present, and reimagined future. (https://www.richmnisi.com/about)

RICH MNISI the brand (on Instagram as @rich_mnisi) presents seasonal clothing collections, as well as handbags and a limited-edition furniture range. The clothing tends towards elaborate colour palettes and patterns combined with slim-fitting, tapered cigarette pants and boldly shaped jackets. The Winter 2021 collection in particular pays explicit homage to queer pride and freedom (as per the deconstructed military dazzle bomber jacket modelled by Karabo Poppy Moletsane in Figure 4.3). Rich Mnisi, the designer, is an out and proud gay man and his personal Instagram account @therichmnisi features many glossy portraits celebrating his handsome face and tall, fit physique, often dressed sexily in his own creations. Although there is much to say about the queer sensibilities of this brand in general, in this section I would like to focus on two key items designed by Mnisi, which although sumptuous and extravagant in shape and styling, are made from monochromatic dark leather.

First up, is a range of black leather handbags. The series of photographs included in the Instagram post from 2 September 2020, show a dark-skinned nude model, Jenyo Johnson, posing against a black studio background, holding the Rich Mnisi handbags in various statuesque, geometric poses (Figure 4.3). The colour palette of the styling is striking: the magnificent smooth skin of the model almost blends into the inky background, the lighting accentuating the similarity between the patina of his skin and that of the leather handbag that he holds, the cool light catching both the curve of his muscle and that of the purse. If it was not a queer Black man who owned the brand that was presenting this level of objectification in the image, there might be cause for critique (see Carolin, 2019; Disemelo, 2015 for detailed discussions of how white gay media objectify Black bodies), but here the visual

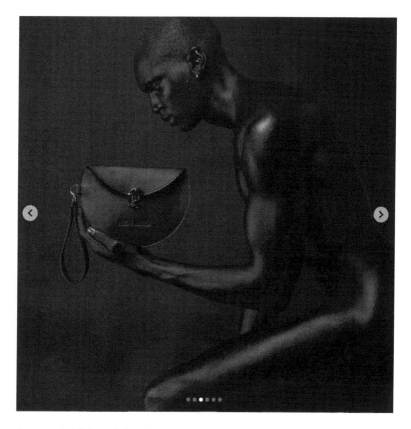

Figure 4.3 Rich Mnisi's Black Leather Handbag, as posted on Instagram. Fair use of publicy shared image.

metonymy in which the commodity and the body are suggested as aligned, if not interchangeable, demands to be read through a queer lens. An altogether different narrative of Black African masculinity is offered in this image, which transcends the objectification argument. Although on the one hand, the body of the model is certainly being offered up for sexual consumption by any number of desiring gazes (as the comment, "These purses ... and this man! Oooooo" evidences), the loving possessive gesture in which the model holds the bag suggests that he is being styled as more than simply a prop for its promotion, but as a desiring user of it himself. Of course, the luxury fashion industry is famously queer friendly (Geczy and Karaminas, 2020; Vänskä, 2014) and it is not unusual for androgynous models to bend gender norms (Blake, 2019) or to be depicted in advertising (Cowart and Wagner, 2021; Soldow, 2013). In this advert, the ordinarily feminized object of the handbag (Rosenberg et al., 2020) is redeployed as available for the use of not only an androgynous subject, but a muscly and masculine fashionista. Mnisi follows an existing, well-established set of norms in the fashion industry (queering subjectivity in relation to commodities), yet takes it further by explicitly putting masculinity into the picture. The bold over-emphasis of black tones, in background, body, and the leather of the bag, speaks to a sensibility in which Black pride in the form of a luxurious, minimalist celebration of ebony skin tones is merged with celebratory queer consumerism.

A similar sensibility is evident in the Nwa-Mulamula Chaise Longue, which Mnisi created as his first foray into furniture design (Figure 4.4). Commissioned by the high-end design gallery, Southern Guild, the piece was nominated as one of South Africa's "most beautiful objects" to the Design Indaba. The flowing curves of the sofa resist clear categorization, though Mnisi says that it is inspired by the shape of an ancestral maternal body (Nwa-mulamula means "guardian"). Mnisi insists, on his web page detailing the inspiration for

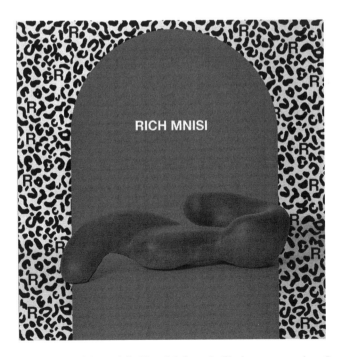

Figure 4.4 Rich Mnisi's Nwa-Mulamula Chaise, as posted on Instagram. Fair use of publicy shared image.

the chaise, that it is a "physical representation" of his "late great-grandmother, [...] the ever-present guardian, whose teachings live on through storytelling generation after generation" (https://www.richmnisi.com/furniture-1). The chaise is accompanied by a footstool standing on "golden puddles" which represent her tears. Accompanying this explanation are images of androgynous bodies clad in leotards nuzzled into semi-foetal positions on the floor, which are offered as a visual reference point for the shape of the chaise. As fellow designer Lukhanyo Mdingi, who nominated the piece, comments: it feels "visceral" and seems to integrate "self and object." Considering the broader sexiness of Mnisi's oeuvre, and his clear and explicit commitment to LGBTQIA+ identity politics and emancipation through fashion, once again it is appropriate to read the Nwa-Mulamula Chaise with "a queer eye" (Sender, 1999).

Although the reference to a sleeping or resting body is clear, the dark navy blue (almost black) leather also suggests a seamless, futuristic aesthetic, perhaps reminiscent of a huge silicone sex toy, or a space-age obsidian airship. Leather is linked to queer masculinities, for example, in the subcultures of leathermen (Mosher et al., 2006) and folk of all genders who give and take "hard" sexualities, for example through BDSM play (Declue, 2016). Writing of Grace Jones, a fashion-forward androgyne who wore leather to great effect (and indeed, famously sang of "warm leatherette"), it has been remarked that her gender ambiguity allowed her to "outmacho the leather set" (Hilderbrand, 2013), which is one reason that she was so wildly popular with gay audiences. Similarly, I argue that Mnisi's graceful, sexy, and minimalist black leather aesthetic outfemmes leather. The chaise is queer in that it resists easy categorization as either masculine or feminine, and is subversively both masculine and feminine, and neither. It features sensuous curves that might be read as feminine, but which could also be referenced as masculine, if one recalls the curves of the model's muscles and handbag shown in Figure 4.3. The dark navy-blue leather suggests both fetish textures (Schroeder and Borgerson, 2012) and a classic understated, masculine materiality, humorously echoed by the dildo-esque protrusions. The imposing size suggests that the piece of furniture is sure to dominate any room in which it is placed. The chaise is given a queer twist that re-feminizes it specifically within the domain of what Katlego Disemelo, inverting Judith Halberstam's famous coda, calls masculine femininity (Disemelo, 2019b: 233). The shape of the chaise – obviously designed for lounging and sitting in various postures of recline and leisure – also implies a wide range of possible surfaces for sexual action and interaction. In keeping with its naming as a guardian, perhaps people who purchase the sofa imagine it keeping them, their bodies and desires, and those of their lovers, safe. As such, as well as feeling queer, the chaise could also be read as a sex-positive luxury object.

None of these readings are foregrounded by the designer, who repeats in various media interviews that the chaise is "simply" an ode to his ancestor. Putting the chaise into dialogue with the rest of Mnisi's oeuvre invites a sexualized, queer reading of the piece, which does not necessarily have to be at odds with a loving respect for one's great-grandparent. Indeed, apart from the creator of a text not having power over how that text is interpreted, there is something profound about the bringing together of a queer sensibility in a luxury object with pride in one's genetic and cultural forebears, as in itself a form of progressive politics. To further theorize Rich Mnisi's design work in dialogue with the brand messages of Karabo Poppy, I turn now to an integrative discussion of the ways in which queer modalities and identities intersect with African luxury brands.

Surfacism and Luxe Performativity

In the examples presented so far in this chapter, we can see that queer identities and sensibilities are harnessed into the project of making African luxury brands. Conversely and connectedly, queer modalities are deployed to add allure to certain commodities. As such, the centrality of Africannness to queer identities, and in turn of queerness to African identities needs further discussion and exploration. Many other scholars have considered, in the kind of detail that is neither possible nor necessary here, how the wide range of human genders and sexualities that exist are perfectly compatible with African cultures and identities (Matebeni et al., 2018; Nyong'o, 2012). Indeed, it may well be the case that the imposition of western, capitalist Christian values through colonialism is a key source for the rejection of queer identities and practices in some African contexts (McEwen, 2019). What I want to explore here is the role that luxury branding as a discourse and modality plays in African queer consumer cultures, and vice versa. Despite the persistence of certain afro-patriarchal discourses that suggest a gulf between queer lives and African traditions and cultures (such fictions being deployed as a basis for violence), this chapter has shown how some African luxury designers use their platforms to promote an alternative narrative that centres queerness in their experiences of being African, and vice versa. Luxury becomes both form and content through which the harmony between African and queer identities is performed and displayed. There are two dimensions to the ways in which queer modalities are deployed in luxury performativity. The first has to do with how shine is used to express empowerment, and make claims for equality. The second has to do with the ways in which brands then appropriate queer shine in an effort to seem relevant and capture loyalty and spending from queer consumers. Both these forms of shine gesture towards imagined futures, or rather, futures actively being built through creative and activist work that are inclusive and have transcended the aesthetic and political limitations of bigotry, heteronormativity, and other forms of oppression, injury, and marginalization based on gender and sexuality.

"A beautiful queer narrative": Pride and Luxury Shine

> Shine is a key element in the self-fashioning and representation of queerness right from the start of modernism and cannot be divorced from what has so far been seen as the mainstream of modernism. In other words, the queer appropriation of shine tells an alternative history of glamour, glitter, and gleam, which must be acknowledged as central to modernism as an alternative, positive and empowering aesthetic strategy.
>
> (Krause-Wahl et al., 2021: 15)

Shine has a history; so too does it have a future and is mobilized into a politics of futurity. Writing in the context of queer (or better, quare) Latinx migrants into the US, Juan D. Ochoa writes that self-fashioning aesthetic work serves the project of making existence legible, for people to no longer hide in the shadows but instead to "shine bright like a diamond" (Ochoa, 2015: 193). When a queer subject, marginalized by migration, the deprival of documentation, or oppressive violence within a society, intentionally finds ways to shine, the political significance is clear. To shine is to do more than state, "I exist." It is to claim that existence is not only the site of resistance but also of pleasure, and these are resources that must be mobilized into any politics of seeking safety, recognition, and inclusion in society. It is significant that this practice of shining bright – also articulated as the "right to be fabulous" (Disemelo, 2021: 264) – is expressed through the modalities of fashion and adornment. This has particular importance in the context of queer subjectivity in Africa. My contribution to these areas of thinking is to show that luxury seems to carry a special meaning in the celebration of queer shine. In his ethnographic study of drag pageants in Johannesburg, Katlego Disemelo shows how the acquisition and sharing of gowns, make-up, and the other accoutrements of glamorous stage presence are the objects of both competition and collaboration for the queens. In their self-presentation online, the drag queens align themselves with luxury objects as part of their claim to fame, which co-constructs their success offline as well as on-stage (Disemelo, 2021). Luxury brands created by Black queer people build on existing affiliations and aspirations toward luxury (which are evident in both queer and non-queer communities), but deploy them in special ways.

Returning to the argument about the political importance of shine to queer subjectivity, it is worth considering how shine operates in the case studies explored in this chapter.

In the case of Karabo Poppy, this happens primarily through the presentation of a globally legible urban aesthetic, in which the city is shown to be at once African and a pleasurable, profitable home for queer artistic praxis and life. The city is the setting that allows queer creativity to shine. Her portraits often show Moletsane outside, in the sunny environs of the city, with sun pouring onto her face and skin. Like this she is illuminated, but she also glows from within with pride and a joyful presentation of herself as an androgynous dyke. Moletsane's "big dyke energy" (BDE) is loud and proud, it wears designer sneakers, and takes for granted its right to be amongst the streets and skyscrapers of Johannesburg, her chosen home city. Although it is not necessarily the "done" dyke thing, to be glittery and "fabulous," with many masculine presenting queer women preferring a more low-key aesthetic, I read Moletsane's smooth, assertive and sexy BDE as functioning to make one aspect of gay pride shine. As Rebecca Coleman argues in her book, *Glitterworlds*, sparkly modalities allow for a particular modulation of queer politics. Where glitter-bombing is used to highlight the existence of homophobic politicians in the streets of American cities (Coleman, 2020), queer subjects also use glitter to highlight and celebrate their own queerness, and to dress their existence with joy, thereby directly repudiating the negation of the bigoted. Although Moletsane does not use glitter per se, it perhaps being too kitsch for her look, choosing instead sunshine, street art, and hand drawn thick marker line as her expressive materials, she similarly aesthetically highlights and celebrates the queerness of her existence. Writing about queer performance artists who use social media, Katlego Disemelo points out that Instagram is seen by some queer creatives as a way to market themselves, but also as "a medium through which to narrate and perform their multifaceted identities" (Disemelo, 2019b: 233), that it is, in the words of Desire Marea (see next section), a "storytelling medium, [...] a way to write a very beautiful queer narrative for ourselves" (Desire Marea, quoted in Disemelo, 2019b: 233). The desire to create a "beautiful queer narrative" is not something unique to artists, or indie creatives (Desire Marea is an alt-pop musician and performance artist, who has recently gained a niche following after the global success of their single, *Tavern Kween*). Commercial artists, such as Karabo Poppy, also use Instagram to create "a beautiful queer narrative," and this beautiful queerness is deployed in order to build brands as well as sell affiliated and associated commodities.

There is a special kind of shine that catches black leather, and this takes centre stage in the Rich Mnisi works discussed in this chapter. Although black and dark surfaces usually absorb light, when they are polished, shiny, oiled, and/or smooth, they catch just enough light to reflect some of it back. The communicative power of such surfaces, when used in advertising, recall fetish sub-cultures (Schroeder and Borgerson, 2012). "Black [...] is a racial category; blackness in semiotic terms connotes exoticized identity and a sexualized fascination with the other [...] in part due to black skin's exoticisation by the Western world" (Schroeder and Borgerson, 2012: 67). Although there might be an intended or unintended deployment of these stereotypical associations with Blackness in the use of smooth, fetish-like black and dark surfaces in Mnisi's luxury objects, arguably there is a more poignant and overt re-appropriation taking place. When Black, queer luxury designers use fetish-like patinas and reference points, they foreground a non-objectifying sexuality. The palette and styling of the Mnisi handbag shoot is reminiscent of the self-portraits of celebrated queer fine arts photographer, Zanele Muholi (Muholi, 2020), particularly her *Somnyama Ngonyama, Hail the Dark Lioness* series (Muholi, 2018). Muholi's use of monochrome photography allows for emphasis to be placed on the specific way that light illuminates Black skin tones. This, along with a styling choice to emphasize by darkening the darkness of Black skin, is key to Muholi's style and seems an explicit reference point for Mnisi's handbag series. In both Muholi's portraiture, and Mnisi's promotional imagery for his luxury products, specifically the handbag, a new politics of luxury surfacism, one that both speaks back to colonial stereotype and utterly transcends it, is evident. The smooth and shiny modalities of Black skin – and all the reference points to it, including dark leather – is celebrated as the ultimate, most precious luxury. In direct opposition to the sexualized commodification that is suggested by glitter, for example, in the exoticized stage presence of Josephine Baker (Cheng, 2011a; Staszak, 2015), the luxurious modality of Black shine is one that is fully reclaimed by queer consuming subjectivities, in the shape of Rich Mnisi's brand. I call this reappropriation of the fetishistic sheen "luxury surfacism": the deployment of a pride-full, Black patina in order to speak back to, and utterly ignore, racist, sexist, and homophobic narratives of glossy modalities.

In both iterations – Moletsane's city gleam and Mnisi's Black surfacism – we see new modalities of African queerness "shining," that is, presenting and expressing itself as not simply valid, but superior to the ordinary. I mean this both in terms of "ordinary" sexualities and ordinary forms of consumption. The high-end luxury commodity, be it the designer bomber jacket, the 1 of 1 AF-1, the handbag, or the sexy chaise longue, has been recruited into the discourse of queer shine. And in turn, the alluring power of queer sexiness builds the luxury brand, both through the creation of a safe, liberating space for queer consumers to celebrate their own, and through the promotion of a progressive, inclusive politics: everyone should have the chance to shine. Tavia Nyong'o names this afro-fabulation: "the persistent reappearance of that which was never meant to appear, but was instead meant to be kept outside or below representation" (Nyong'o, 2018: 3). The joyful, glamorous, and luxurious narratives offered by queer, Black African creative subjects like Karabo Poppy and Rich Mnisi are examples of this persistently political choice to appear: to shine.

Selling Queer Creativity? Capitalism with/against Queer Emancipation

So far, I have shown how certain African luxury brands deploy various loud and proud queer sensibilities as part of a project of archiving queer culture in real time, as well as in the joyful expression of artistic ideas, selves, and sexualities. The corollary to this is that queer creatives, including those firmly situated within the commercial realms of fashion, furniture, and graphic design, see luxury as integral to the promotion of their identities online. Luxury therefore needs to be understood as a key modality of Black African queer self-empowerment, which I have summarized as shine, and which is expressed in urban and textural forms. This is a largely optimistic narrative: that selves can be forged, liberated, and celebrated through the performance of a luxury commodity-saturated, urban consumer lifestyle. Without taking away from the important modes of self-fashioning and expression that luxury consumer culture offers queer people, it is nevertheless also important to consider whether, and if so how, the wholesale integration of neoliberal attitudes and economies are in synch with the "queer agenda," which is "grounded in the knowledge that the issues queer and trans people face are a product of the overlapping systems of neo-liberal capitalism, global White supremacy, and heterosexism" (Jones et al., 2018: 10). From the perspective of critical gender and race theory, the concept of "queer" is inherently at odds with capitalism, which is framed as the source and site of oppression and thus requires dismantling. Can capitalism be queer? Does queering capitalism simply mean bringing queer ethics and aesthetics into existing forms of commodity exchange, or remaking those altogether? And, as an integral part of the capitalist economy, can luxury be queer or vice versa?

As this chapter has shown, the answer cannot be one of an either-or binary. Queer culture and the attendant politics of visibility interacts with commercial capitalism in complex ways. The two ideological framings, while by no means equivalent and deploying power equally, do not cancel one another out. "Queer subjects" can enhance "their autonomy vis-à-vis local heteronormative traditions by creative engagements that take advantage of opportunities provided by the growth of the market economy" (Jackson, 2009: 356). As the cases offered in this chapter illustrate, queer luxury brand messaging can offer an inclusive vision of African design, one in which avant-garde luxury aesthetics and queer pride sit comfortably with narratives of cultural heritage, and all are welcome to use (buy) the resources offered in order to "shine." The personal brands of creatives who in their self-presentation and creative production write against the over-styled, faux-glossy, kitsch aesthetics of mass-market branding shows how the avant-garde of African luxury branding offers a new sensibility. Queer creatives may be destined to become the most lucrative and influential creators of luxury coming from the continent. I have written elsewhere about how global luxury brands and consultants see African markets as a "last frontier" (Iqani, 2019) that needs to be conquered. It could well be that queer consumers are seen as the new frontier within that last frontier. As individuals find ways to empower themselves economically and culturally, and move to cities, they may increasingly desire luxury commodities, especially those that are "for us by us." As such, the increasing visibility of queerness within the African luxury sector augurs new cultures of consumption and aspiration, and queer creatives that tap into this aspirational market are acting with autonomy, and taking advantage of market opportunities for their own benefit, and by extension the benefit of the communities that they represent and care about.

Figure 4.5 offers a useful example of the complexities of the ways in which commercialism and queer emancipatory politics come together in African luxury branding. Desire Marea is an upcoming alt-pop

Figure 4.5 Desire Marea X Calvin Klein – who is selling whose shine? ©
Desire Marea, reproduced with their kind permission.

music star, who is well-known in the queer performance scene in
South Africa, Johannesburg specifically, and is starting to gain some
international recognition. Marea is one half of the duo, FAKA, and
has an individual presence online and in the clubs. As Katlego
Disemelo has written, FAKA's style when they were starting out was,
"unapologetically kitsch 90s aesthetic [...] juxtaposed with a chic and
street-savvy trendiness" (Disemelo, 2019b) and it was not uncommon
to see the duo "barge through classist gallery spaces with their torn
fishnet stockings, cheap synthetic wigs, a mix of loud gqom-techno
music and lascivious dance moves" (Disemelo, 2019b: 227). In this
portrait posted to Instagram by Marea, we certainly see some traces
of the "ghetto-chic" (Disemelo, 2019b: 227) aesthetic, in the long

synthetic wig, and the hoop earrings. In the lavish double-breasted leather coat, cinched in at the waist by no less than two buckled belts, we see a nod to a Mnisi-style surfacism, and certainly a sense of pleasurable excess: in short, luxury. Marea's flawless matte make-up offers a further sense of shine, and the only skin visible outside the geometric silhouette of the dramatic coat is their face, which glows sensuously. The sense of drama is produced by glamorous red lighting, reminiscent of the nightclub or stage, which reflects sexily off the leather patina. Marea poses in front of a blank wall, which is decorated by the shadows thrown by the red light, deepening the dramatic effect. But perhaps the most striking thing about the post is that it is a "paid partnership" with an advertising agency, and Marea presents a bottle of Calvin Klein Everyone cologne. The promotion of brands and commodities is one key way in which creatives can monetize their online presence. Be they influencers or celebrities, the deployment of a personal social media platform as a site for niche advertising is certainly a key feature of millennial media culture (Freberg et al., 2011; Iqani, 2021; Khamis et al., 2017). Arguably, Marea is, in this kind of post, rightfully profiting off his own image and self-presentation, and shrewdly finding ways to turn the attention economy into real income. It is equally arguable, however, that this image represents a kind of selling out of the queer agenda, or at least, an uncritical buying in to global brand culture. While there is a history of including and even celebrating queer aesthetics in advertising (Campbell, 2015; Kates, 1999), it is important to ask who is seeking to benefit off whose shine (Figure 4.5).

There is a certain prestige for a local queer artist, like Desire Marea, in being visibly associated with a global luxury brand, which has in the past commissioned elite celebrities as brand ambassadors. The association with a global luxury brand sends a message of arrival and recognition, and a legitimation of their creative output and influence with an audience. Yet, CK could be seen as attempting to appropriate a sense of authenticity by associating themselves with Marea, who has established a following through an original, rebellious creative practice, that sought to shock and bother the artistic establishment, through "performances of disidentification that create subversive meaning within the alienating context of neoliberal white supremacist consumer capitalist heteropatriarchy" (Disemelo, 2019b: 226). Although there are some queer traces in CK's advertising (De Bortoli, 2018), it remains an elite global brand that surely must be understood to be a part of the system of global consumer capitalism, that Marea and FAKA used to actively seek to interrupt with their queer agenda. Discussing the study of commercialized sexiness and non-normative sexual identities and practices, it has been observed that "it is not enough simply to add queer and stir" (Smith, 2015: 13). The same can certainly be said of the study of luxury branding – it is not simply enough for global brands to add local, queer imagery, and "stir." I do not want to unduly critique Marea's choice to partner with CK: in the gig economy of the creative sector, and the ongoing hustle many creatives must undertake in order to earn enough to pay for their living costs and continue to make their work, such deals can be lucrative while also allowing a lot of say over how they are presented (as is evident from the choices Marea made in the styling, photography, and captioning of the paid partnership). What is revealed by the post is an issue bigger than its specifics: the extent to which luxury branding (in general in terms of the operations of powerful global companies, and specifically in terms of emerging African labels) and queer culture are compatible. Desire Marea's alliance, albeit temporary, with a global luxury fashion brand, indicates that there are complex interlacings of queer visibility and the ways in which commercial power tries to assimilate radical culture.

The African luxury sector is at the forefront of a new debate between queer commercialism and queer theory. No matter how "woke" and even when owned and championed by a Black queer creative, any business must keep profit as its main goal otherwise it will cease to exist. As such, we must ask whether the integration of queer ideas into commercial communication inherently dilutes the emancipatory politics of queer culture and queer theory. Similarly, we could consider the extent to which the entry of African queer creatives into the luxury sector, be it through the creation of their own lines and brands, or their purposive partnering with global brands, might in fact represent a genuine shift in the dynamics of power, and a claiming of economic agency and markets "for us, by us." This brings us to a consideration of the ways in which homonormativity (Duggan, 2020) might integrate with luxury commercialism. Although in the brand messages and aesthetic content of the case studies discussed here we have seen the joyful presentation of all sorts of queer ideas – from big dyke energy to fetishistic subcultures – these are mediated through the modalities of consumer culture. In short, the queer values celebrated have price tags attached: be it the $1,000 estimated cost of the 1 of 1 custom AF-1 or the $25,000 chaise longue.

Is commercial practice always inherently exploitative, even when it is enthusiastically chosen by marginalized or previously marginalized groups as a way to improve lives or advance communities? There is validity to the critical, Marxist-inspired complaint about the manner in which capital always extracts value from workers and citizens and forces them into increasingly individualized silos, from which it is increasingly difficult to forge solidarity and communities of care. Yet, as shown by the visual forms and meanings attached to queer African luxury brands, commercial forms of knowledge production and expression do deserve to be seen as valid sites from which non-normative ideas have the potential to be celebrated in ways meaningful to those making that choice.

Many groups and individuals who have been historically excluded from mainstream economies and opportunities to build wealth consider the ability to consume freely (or at least, more freely than before) to be a key indicator of progress towards equality and inclusion (Iqani, 2015, 2016; Iqani and Kenny, 2017). This is particularly the case in neo-liberal societies, such as South Africa (and other global south countries such as India and Brazil) where the state uses a rhetoric of social welfare while systematically eroding and stripping away public institutions, increasingly placing the responsibility for personal growth and wellbeing, welfare, and advancement, upon individual efforts. The discourse of "making it" is an outcome of this state of affairs: where individuals aspire to better lives but are not provided with the public resources (good education, healthcare, urban infrastructures) in order to do so, they are left to hustle their lonely ways through an inhospitable landscape in their quests (or dreams) to have and be more and to provide opportunities for their families.

It is important to not paint all queer folk with the same brush: heterogeneity of ideology and political opinion is always intrinsically a part of any "group." Some queer folk might be committed free-market capitalists while others may believe firmly in socialist approaches to organizing the economy. As this chapter has shown, many queer folk are excellent businesspeople, and have crafted successful designer brands both on the basis of their openly queer sensibilities, their design and artistic excellence, and smart promotional communications. Like many other cultural resources, the messages, ideologies, and politics of queerness are being harnessed into luxury commercial projects, and in turn commercialism is being centred in some queer lives. Although at its heart, queer theory is about emancipation from the strict gender structures that are associated with white supremacist capitalist patriarchy, capitalism has also shown itself to be more than willing to integrate and appropriate radical ideas and aesthetics into its promotional discourses. So too, should it be acknowledged that many queer African individuals are deeply embedded in capitalist practices, and may not see profit-oriented, luxury, commercial activities as in any way contradictory to their sexual preferences and identities.

5 From Soft Power to Queer Futures: New Directions for African Luxury

This chapter brings together the focused and detailed analytical discussions offered in the previous three chapters, by reflecting on the cross-cutting and over-arching theoretical issues that all the case studies indicate.

First, I show how the six case studies and three themes that were presented are interrelated in ways more complex than separate discussions could possibly represent. In short, all of the case studies discussed in this book show aspects of celebration of cultural heritage, an appreciation of the natural, and forward-looking values. My contribution to luxury scholarship and indeed African cultural studies (at the interface of which two fields of enquiry this book is positioned) is that African luxury branding as a genre of promotional communication should be understood to be built upon these three discursive strategies that harness narratives of culture, nature, and future.

Second, I build on these observations to show how African luxury branding operates through a complex dialectic of global and local, and show how this dynamic is related to, and extends, existing theories of the operations of luxury discourse. The argument is that being both and neither purely African and global allows luxury brands coming from the Continent to cleverly explode old stereotypes and forge new ways to participate in international aesthetic economies. This fusion of culture and market allows for a deeper consideration of how luxury is a site where aesthetics and economics interconnect in complex ways, always shaped by history, context, and tradition.

Third, the chapter turns to the argument that African luxury brands should be understood to be exemplary creative and cultural industries, and that they are staking a claim for the place of creativity and creative work in African economies and indeed the bigger picture of economic development. This optimistic potential is explored and critiqued.

DOI: 10.4324/9781003227038-5

Finally, the chapter offers a clear-eyed, sobering critique of the extent to which the aesthetics of African luxury branding can play a role in the economic emancipation of African countries and citizens, considering the perpetuation of extractive investment, inequitable trade relations, and the persistent marginalization of African creativity and intellectual property by other powerful economic players. Although much of the analysis in this book has been driven by the optimistic energy that was evident in the practices and discourses of African luxury brands themselves, it is important to temper the idealism, as enjoyable and tempting as it might be to succumb to it completely, with a return to a critical perspective grounded in a realistic assessment of political-economic structures.

Culture, Nature, Future

The previous chapters have demonstrated three key aesthetic strategies and narrative themes used in African luxury branding. The first has to do with *culture*, and reveals how some African luxury designers mine their own heritage and historical aesthetics for inspiration, and remix and re-present selected images and styles from their ancestry and cultural DNA into luxury products. Although these are intended as the proud and joyful celebration of cultural heritage, and the right to turn it into expensive commodities is claimed as an inheritance, the luxury products embodying that inheritance are offered on the open market for any person, from any background to buy and enjoy. The second has to do with *nature*, and shows how some African luxury entrepreneurs reach to organic substances and a communion with the natural world for both inspiration and materials, and align these aesthetics with both pre-colonial and anti-colonial politics, which take shape in ways that have specific relevance to feminine subjectivities. The third has to do with *future*, and shows how some African designers engage a variety of queer textures and imagery in their work, which hints at an Afro-futuristic vision of beautiful emancipation both embedded in and partially resisting capitalist structures of power and pleasure. Taken together, the luxury narratives of cultura, nature, and future can be seen as projecting a utopian African vision of an alternative to colonial-capitalism, and in critique of existing inequity in social formations and representations.

For analytical reasons, and to fully explicate the qualitative specifics of each of these themes, I have presented them in separate chapters, with detailed discussion of specifically chosen examples. The sensibilities of culture, nature, and future in African luxury branding are not mutually exclusive. It is certainly the case that futuristic brands also openly draw on personal and cultural heritage, while naturalistic brands also speak implicitly to ideals of environmentally sustainable futures. And although the aesthetics of cultural brands clearly draw on and celebrate certain aspects of heritage, through their re-mixing of those cultural codes, they are implicitly re-writing the past into aesthetics that are relevant not only to the present but also the future: an Afrotopia in which African cultural heritage stands on par with, and has equal value to, other global luxury brands. Although for the purposes of this book I have purposefully organized case studies into particular categories, there are of course important overlaps and conversations between the case studies and analytical themes. I do not intend the case studies that I have offered – Thebe Magugu, The Herd in relation to cultural heritage, Gugu Intimates and Suki Suki Naturals in relation to natural sensibilities, Rich Mnisi and Karabo Poppy in relation to queer futures – to be read as somehow excluding any re-altion to the other themes. In fact, each case study can be said to speak to the other two themes as well as to the one that it was deployed to spotlight. Thebe Magugu, for example, includes queer iconography and futuristic aesthetics in many of his designs, and often reaches for natural landscapes as a backdrop for shoots. The Herd deploys geo-graphical motifs as much as historical heritage narratives in its pre-sentation of its brand values. Rich Mnisi is known to celebrate a nude skin-centric aesthetic in some fashion shoot styling, and often centres a verbal explication of being inspired by his cultural heritage and an-cestors in his design discourse. Gugu Intimates could certainly be read as celebrating homo-erotic love between women, and although Karabo Poppy clearly sees the city as her home, she also prefers neutral, nat-ural forms of self-presentation in relation to her own skin and hair styles. In short, the aesthetic strategies that I have identified in this book are not rigidly associated to the brands through which I have discussed them. This was an analytical choice, and other writers and researchers will discover other meanings that I did not, and will deploy the ideas in relation to these brand images, or others, on their own terms and with their own theoretical frameworks at play. Although I have identified three sensibilities of African luxury branding through the discussion of specific brands, my argument is that these discursive themes and strategies have wider applicability in the study of pro-motional communication coming from African brands and compa-nies (including the personal brands of influencers and celebrities). Although I have focussed to an extent on the individual people at the helm of each brand, they have all surely drawn on a wealth of input from other creative workers in their production and communications. As such, they represent a broader and more complex landscape of cultural production.

In their visual labour and brand communication, the African luxury brands examined in this book stitch together past and future, nature and culture, and aesthetics and politics. The creatives leading these brands intentionally and lovingly mine their own cultural heritage to bring these resources – which were historically plundered and shipped off to European museums – to celebrate their beauty, validity, and spiritual power. The brands succeed in remixing cultural resources to make the past relevant to the present, and of interest to younger generations who may have up to now associated such items and aesthetics with their grandparents or great-grandparents. By bringing these cultural resources into the present, and making them relevant to contemporary consumer markets and sensibilities, African luxury branding is also catapulting them into the future by creating a highly mediated, living archive of heritage and memory that pays tributes not only to the source of their inspiration but their own creative acumen and work. Similarly, by drawing on natural and botanical resources to claim a pared down, minimalist version of African luxury, brands are able to rewrite the historically stereotyping narratives of Africans as close to nature and "primitive," and use the minimalist sensibility to reclaim an authentic connection to and love for the natural as something that is embedded in culture rather than opposed to it, as something that can work for Black African pride, empowerment, and quality of life, rather than against it.

The reclamation of a "back to nature" aesthetic has significance for Black feminine subjectivities in particular, and offers a site through which it is possible to explore a merging of urban sensibilities with rural, the concerns and interests of city dwellers with the natural landscapes of beyond, in both time and place. Instead of the un-peopled landscape that colonial narratives constructed, African luxury brands intentionally people that landscape with women who live in harmony with it, and who deploy their wisdom in relation to its botanical treasures for their own pleasure and profit. From this perspective, "nude" is not just a modality for the sexy selling of feminized commodities, but a political standpoint in which the power and pleasure housed in feminine bodies is activated by the very owners of those bodies, for purposes fully owned and chosen, "for us, by us." This articulates with other rights movements discourses, for example the disability rights community's call regarding, "nothing about us without us" (Scotch, 2009). The deployment of nature discourses connects with both past and future, in terms of referencing pre-colonial idylls as well as promoting anti-colonial (anti-racist, anti-sexist) politics. It also hints at the coming climate apocalypse and the possible (probable) irretrievable loss of natural biodiversity and landscapes as a result, an effect most likely to be felt by those not responsible for the carbon emissions that caused global warming (Yusoff, 2018). In respect of apocalyptic futures, an alternate narrative of beautiful, queer liberation is offered, in which fashionable cyborg-creatures stalk glamorous cities, perhaps hinting at a sci-fi or fantasy version of the future in which all is not lost from overheating, water crises, floods and famine, and queer politics has triumphed to re-forge humanity into an inclusive, caring, responsible species rather than the violent version we know so well.

In considering possible futures that await humanity, the question of what role luxury industries, commodities, and brand cultures might play in that future might seem fanciful, pointless even. But there is arguably validity to a pragmatic approach that foresees consumption and production as remaining somehow relevant to future economies and cultures, come what apocalypse may. Luxury fashion, in particular, might have a role to play in seeking sustainable alternatives to current mass production, wasteful, fast-fashion approaches, as well as to developing products that are more in tune with what nature has the capacity to offer. I return to some of these issues in the final section of this chapter.

Between Global and Local

This book has clearly demonstrated that it is not sufficient to theorize luxury as a western concept, imported to African contexts. Although some commentators might be tempted to label luxury a form of cultural imperialism (Tomlinson, 2012), a new trojan horse of materialism through which western values gain access to, and dominate, African values, the creative and aesthetic labour of African luxury brands proves otherwise. Luxury is as African a resource as it is linked to any other cultural frameworks and background. The Eurocentric perspective on luxury, which seems to have evolved in the luxury literature to date, is flawed for a number of reasons. Firstly, it creates a false dichotomy between western and African value systems, as though both are essential and absolute. In reality of course, and this has been true throughout human history, cultures are dynamic, ever-changing, adaptive, relative, and position themselves against one another in organic ways, and also bleed into one another in surprising ways. Culture is porous, diverse, and hybrid (Bhabha, 2012). This is not to suggest that there has not been an exercise of power by certain cultures over others, as the violent history of colonialism all too clearly evidences, but to highlight that the intermixing of cultural perspectives and value systems is perhaps one of the most pervasive effects of globalization from the very moment that some human ethnicities first came into contact with others. Furthermore, the notions of "Western" and "African" are problematic in that they homogenize existing diversity in conceptually unhelpful ways. Even though I myself have deferred to the shorthand of these descriptors, it is important to pause to reflect on the inadequacy of such categories to capture the full richness and diversity of human culture, creativity and communication. Both the west and the African continent feature a huge diversity of linguistic, religious, ideological, cultural, and social expressions, and suggesting that they are all the same is not only essentializing but overly simplistic, and how these will be expressed in luxury is equally complex and diverse. The argument of western modernization, well critiqued by theories of cultural imperialism (see Hardy, 2014), incorrectly suggests a taken-for-granted hierarchy; that there is a culture that seeks to dominate and one that can be dominated, that the imperial culture considers itself to be better and that the culture taking in the media and other ideological artefacts of that dominator is in some way inferior. Although there are histories of colonialism and oppression and legacies of unjust distributions of resources that shape the extent to which certain cultures are seen and heard on the global stage of media culture, at their heart, all human cultures are equally significant and valuable, acting as diverse expressions of the same, innately human qualities and values that unite the species on a fundamental level.

African luxury brands are, to an extent, built on this essential truth. Although due to the unfair advantage forged for themselves through violent conquest and colonial thievery, the economies of the industrialized west have greater resources to manufacture and export their cultural artefacts around the world, this does not at all translate into them being "better," and it should most certainly not be assumed that all African subjects see them that way, or are willing to abandon their own much-loved and prized cultural expressions in order to acquire western objects. Some notions of cultural domination are problematic (see Golding and Harris, 1996; Hardy, 2014; Roach, 1997; Tomlinson, 2012) in that they ascribe too much power to the cultural artefacts themselves, whether a Disney film or a designer handbag, as being capable of agency and action. In the same way that media effects theory has been debunked, in that it is not the video game itself that can turn a person violent, or pornography that produces a rapist, similarly it cannot be argued that cultural objects, be they luxury or otherwise, have the power to change identity, behaviour, or the deep-seated and much-cherished values and traditions that define the receiving culture. Luxury commodities and brands therefore, cannot be thought of as solely responsible for producing social effects. Rather they should be understood to be just one out of a huge number of social, economic, and political factors that will influence how individuals, communities, and indeed entire nations act and interact. This book argues that the study of luxury in African contexts must consider African cultures and forms of communication to be inherently and qualitatively equal to all other human cultures and forms of communication, and deserving of full respect and critical attention, in their own rights.

Although there are some aspects of African luxury that are unique and deserve highlighting, especially in relation to brands endemic to African economies and societies, this book has shown that to a large extent in African contexts luxury is defined and deployed in ways quite similar to elsewhere in the world. Cultural heritage is prized and highlighted. Craftsmanship and artistry is centred and celebrated. Avant garde creativity and auteur genius is accentuated and admired. This is not to suggest that luxury is a global or globalizing concept, to which African entrepreneurs are subjected, but to highlight how African luxury workers are themselves global and globalizing subjects, in the sense that they are actively and intentionally participating as equals in a global industry and making the claim that their contributions are on par with iterations elsewhere in the world. It would be a mistake to hold on to the binary thinking that situates Africa as somehow outside of the global or modern, and as oppositional in form and content to "the West," which is often used as a stand in for "the global." As other important theorists (Ferguson, 2006; Kupe, 2013; Prestholdt, 2007) have shown, Africa is and always has been part of the global, and African thinkers, writers, artists, and creatives engage with global questions and reference points as much as do agents from elsewhere. The same is true for African luxury creatives, who intentionally mine their own cultural heritages while simultaneously participating in global aesthetic practices and debates, in the packaging of the cultural material they have inherited into desirable and marketable commodities.

The key research question that this book has asked and answered, building on the key arguments emerging from this critical work on luxury in African contexts, is how luxury brands in Africa construct narratives about their originality, value and place in the global consumer economy. Although this is inherently a question about the operations of discourse in the commercial domain, it also contributes to production studies as I have shown how brands working in a particular market use the idea of luxury to create, promote and sell their wares. This cuts into questions of the global cultural economy because of the key links between culture and luxury, in globalized consumer cultures the producers and disseminators of ideas about luxury are also themselves consumers of luxury goods. Thus African luxury brands inherently appeal to a demographic that likely either is transnational in practice or aspires to be. Luxury has been present in a variety of subcultures in Africa for decades (Brodin et al., 2016; Gondola, 1999; Howell and Vincent, 2014). As well as these practices, African luxury branding is a key site for exploring the complexities of social inequality, because luxury goods are extremely visible manifestations of wealth, and it is impossible to theorize inequality without theorizing wealth. As this book has shown, luxury should be theorized as both a tool of power and a tool of empowerment, and as intricately connected to discourse as expressed through communicative forms and practices. The global and local are intertwined and co-construct one another. Local products seek and often find success on global markets, and global brands seek ever new creative resources and references from local cultures and aesthetics. In the work and success of African luxury brands, we see locally owned creative businesses seeking to enter and compete in global markets, and using their localness and their right to use their own cultural resources, as a key communication point. What does this imply for the role that African luxury brands can play in national economic growth?

Creative Industries and Economic Growth

Government discourses and policies about creative and cultural industries acquired a lot of scholarly attention in the 2010s, with good reason (Hesmondhalgh, 2007; Potts and Cunningham, 2008). Critical researchers needed to examine and assess the legitimacy of strategies that seemed to suggest that governments finally understood the cultural and economic importance of creative, media, and cultural industries. Less is known about how such industries function in African contexts, though important research is starting to unpack such questions. While some policy-oriented research exists exploring the role of creative industries in Africa (De Beukelaer, 2017), for example in relation to urban regeneration (Oyekunle, 2017) and film-making and distribution (Jedlowski, 2012, 2017), more work is needed that examines the extent to which African governments create and implement policy and regulation that supports or hinders creative entrepreneurship in general, and in the luxury sector in specific. More broadly, more research is needed that critically examines how luxury entrepreneurs in African contexts work, do business, innovate, and create jobs and products, sometimes in contexts that are not necessarily very conducive to business activities (for example, state power supply is erratic, taxes are high, and/or bureaucracies make certain processes more complex than they need to be).

One thing that should be clear from the discussion offered in this book is that African luxury brands are very important players in the African cultural and creative industries. Working across a variety of sectors, from fashion to body care, from furniture to music and jewellery design, creative entrepreneurs in African contexts are setting up businesses that capitalize not only on the idea of cultural expression but on the creative labours of specifically talented individuals. Further, these businesses are seeking to sell products and services not only to their own local markets, but also globally. It is important to ask – indeed future researchers must – how luxury industries can contribute quantitatively to economic growth of their national economies, and general economic development on the continent as a whole. The luxury sector has significant capacity to create quality jobs, on account of the skilled and time-consuming labour often required to make high-end products, and this could dovetail productively with an existing artisanal talent pool on the continent. The work of luxury entrepreneurship and brands could certainly contribute to the creation of good, well-paying jobs, and to the elevation of African cultural artisanship to globally recognized brands and commodities. Although certain big media companies, like South Africa's television broadcaster Multichoice and telecommunications company MTN have accessed markets on the continent through licences given by governments, questions need to be asked about how smaller companies, as luxury start-ups tend to be, can get similar governmental support in order to grow their operations and contribute effectively to their national economies. This cannot necessarily happen on the power of entrepreneurial effort alone, governments need to create an enabling and rewarding business environment, which needs to integrate an understanding of the economic potential of the cultural and creative industries. Given the track record of many African governments, it might seem wildly idealistic to think that luxury creative industries will receive the regulatory and policy support that they need to thrive. It may well be the case that many African luxury brands that are achieving success are doing so in spite of state infrastructures and policies, rather than with their assistance.

Future research on African luxury brands and companies should monitor and map, longitudinally if possible, their contributions to economic growth and job creation, and the growth of their market share in the global luxury industry. Further, more detailed studies are needed on labour in African luxury industries, and the extent to which existing power structures may help or hinder equity in this particular sub-genre of work. As this book has shown, women and queer creatives are key to the "rise" of African luxury, and such, questions about the safety of women and LGBTQIA+ people in African contexts may well be central to the future of the African luxury sector. In order to have ideas and create new concepts, companies, commodities, and brands, people need to be safe and well and not under threat of violence and intimidation, as many African women and queer folk are. As such, when asking what social, cultural and political structures African governments can and should put in place to ꞏsupport ongoing innovation, equality of opportunity in relation to gender and sexuality is a central issue, and its neglect should be considered a major threat to one possible avenue of African economic development. Nevertheless, it is important to acknowledge and indeed theorize the optimism and idealism that underlies the enthusiastic narratives about the role that luxury can play in economic growth. While the luxury industry is of course unashamedly neoliberal in that free market trade and individualistic economic activity are centred, there remains the potential for collective welfare and quality of life improvement to be linked into African luxury branding. On one level this is discursive, as this book has shown, but there are also material aspects to the growth in African luxury industries that could have broader economic benefit, not least the quality jobs created and the families and communities supported by the people employed in those jobs. African economies, their growth or decline, their management or mis-management, is the subject of a huge swathe of economic and political research. Future work should explore how luxury industries fit therein, and critical humanities approaches should consider the broader cultural ramifications of their operations and success for societies that are famed as highly unequal (Francis et al., 2020), and which are continuing to grow in inequality.

Constraints on African Economic Freedom

This book has shown how African luxury branding is one avenue through which narratives of Africa as a place of beauty, hope, talent, and wealth are gaining traction. This form of "soft power" needs to be considered in context. As has been noted, there is real potential for economic growth and job creation linked to the establishment and operations of African luxury brands, although these are likely to be miniscule compared to other industries such as mining, tourism, and finance (though indeed, luxury can be linked to all three). As globally connected Africans split their time between their African and American or European homes, and facilitate new forms of exchange and trade between the west and African economies, and as African elites and middle classes continue to strive for the pleasurable qualities of life that every human being has a right to desire, it is likely that there will be significant growth in an affiliation towards luxury on the continent. Home grown luxury brands see this potential and seek to supply luxurious high-end designer products to meet the growing demands both for elite consumption opportunities and for connecting with African pride and developing local economies. As an African myself (a white South African of Middle Eastern ancestry, but nevertheless a committed citizen of this continent), it is difficult to not get a little bit excited about the creative and development potential of a sector that seems – on account of its own self-promotion and branding at least – to be doing quite well. Might luxury actually offer one potential pathway out of the gross inequality that is evident across the global south, and in South Africa in particular? Dare we hope that the manufacture of highly expensive objects for the few might create more good, secure, and enjoyable jobs for the many? Might we imagine new creative, local economies emerging that honour and champion indigenous knowledges, cultures, and expertize, and see forms of profit created that flow directly back to the people and communities that have inherited those riches?

This book has explored the optimistic aspects of African luxury branding, because it is impossible to ignore the optimism that is threaded into the promotional discourses of African luxury brands. As such, this book stands in some ways as a celebration of the creative ingenuity and wily strategic communication of some of the brilliant, creative business people who are making things happen on the African luxury scene. But it is necessary to temper some of this celebratory feeling with a more cautious assessment of the political and economic structures that may limit the positive potential of the sector. From the macro-economic perspective, African economies suffer from many challenges (Asongu and Odhiambo, 2019), including formal financial regulations inhibiting to small businesses, unstable infrastructure, poor tax collection combined with high tax rates for small sectors of the formally employed population, corruption and mismanagement of public funds, high levels of unemployment, massive national debt, and unfavourable loan conditions from the global financial agencies. This raises the question of whether, and if so how, the luxury cultural economy can be an engine of progress, or whether it merely exacerbates existing inequalities. Although it is neither possible nor necessary to go into depth about these issues here, it is worth noting that these are the product of the history and concomitant contemporary relation of global balances of power (see Cramer et al., 2020). Colonial extraction and oppression was hugely destructive to the African continent, and the legacies of this brutal history are still evident. The countries that benefitted from racist economic exploitation remain stronger, richer, and more influential in global politics and trade. African countries, despite huge youthful populations with massive reserves of talent and potential, simply lack the economies of scale and political influence to compete on equal terms with America and the EU, and increasingly, China. Furthermore, there has been a trend of self-serving, autocratic governance in many African states, with a corrupt elite clinging to power and using it to self-enrich rather than achieve broad-based improvements in quality of life (Ganahl, 2014). Many African governments have allowed infrastructure key to economic functioning, such as the provision of power and clean water, to crumble through neglect and mismanagement, and this has a massive knock on effect for any business operation. Some have argued that the world is evolving towards Africa (Comaroff and Comaroff, 2012), that a coming collapse, be it economic in the ways predicted by Marx and speeded up by financial markets gambling, or environmental as climate catastrophe looms, will mean that the West will have to learn to live with precarity, broken infrastructures, uncertainty, and fear. The Comaroffs' argument is that because Africans already know how to not only survive, but sometimes thrive, with these conditions, that African states of being may soon become the norm, thereby giving Africa a head start on the politics of futurity. This argument, although compelling in its apocalypsism, still relies on a binary of West vs Rest (Hall, 2020). I argue that it is more productive to consider the Global South not as a place, but as a condition of fragment, contradiction, and complexity (Hofmeyr, 2014), and which always holds some features of the global north within it, as does the Global North always include some features of the south. Is it sensible to think of luxury as relative to the global south, or should it be integrated into our thinking about what the global north means, and how it bifurcates across geography, and is always evident in every society?

It would be a mistake to argue that African luxury brands are equivalent to those emanating from the West. Although they are aesthetically and ethically of equal intrinsic value – the Afro-centric or biased amongst us might claim that they are *more* beautiful, morally sound – they are not playing on an equal pitch. Instead of supportive regulatory and economic conditions, such as those enjoyed by luxury businesses in the West, and the benefit of supportive environments having been actively cultivated for several decades, African luxury businesses are working in difficult conditions. As well as the significant challenges posed by the ordinary business processes of design, manufacture, and marketing, businesses owners in African contexts (be they creative or otherwise) also have to battle with scheduled and unscheduled power cuts, poor transport infrastructures, high levels of crime, and other forms of social unrest caused by inequality. Further, they struggle through complex and/or inefficient state systems, where they exist. African luxury goods have the glossy appearances that occlude their conditions of production, which are significantly disadvantaged compared to their competitors in the West. I do not wish to over-emphasize the negative aspects of doing business in African countries and economies, though they are of course present to some extent. African countries also host gleaming cities, effective transport systems both formal and informal, excellent universities and fancy malls. It will be necessary for critical analysts to consider the various ways in which the functional and dysfunctional aspects of African economies and infrastructures help or hinder the workings of African luxury industries. Further, it will be interesting for researchers in both macroeconomic and microeconomic sectors to explore how global trade relations and international exercises of power might influence the creation and operation of African luxury brands. Future research in African luxury branding should take into account the limits to economic growth. Capitalism has proved itself, time and again, as incapable of delivering equality and fairness, of forging social safety nets, of supporting welfare economies, of bringing that better life than so many crave and deserve within reach. Although the optimistic narrative of how luxury businesses can grow economies and create jobs through the making of beautiful things are not without evidence and validity, this needs to be held against the question of what capitalism has actually achieved in African countries today. The answer does not seem to be jobs, equality, justice, and equity.

New Directions?

This book has deployed critical race, feminist, queer, and decolonial visual theories in order to synthesize new perspectives on the role of

Africa in critical luxury studies, and the role of luxury in critical and decolonial African studies of neoliberal power, thus contributing to advancing both areas.

I summarize these new opportunities for research as connecting with three key areas: equity, quality of life, and sustainability.

Concerning equity, this book has shown how African luxury brands are important sites for the creation of new discourses and narratives about equality on the basis of ethnicity, race, gender, and sexuality. These discourses speak back to representational power rooted in colonialism, and forge new modalities of meaning through the deployment of uniquely African communicative resources, linked culture, nature, and future. From soft power to queer futurism, African luxury branding voices a powerful claim to the beauty and significance of creative work rooted in and transcending the continent. Future researchers interested in the links between luxury and equity may wish to ask how the discursive strategies and narrative approaches of African luxury branding connect with and diverge from the promotional communications of luxury branding elsewhere on the globe, especially across the Global South, as well as how luxury as an industry and set of values can or does contribute to lowering inequality through job creation. Further, it will be important to ask how the politics of gender and sexual equality in the continent intersects with the broadening of the consumer sector through luxury, and how in turn oppression of women and queer people may indeed limit opportunities for consumer market access and growth.

Concerning quality of life, this book has foregrounded how African luxury brands highlight the importance of joy and happiness to self-expression and self-actualization. It is well established in the critical literature on consumption that material goods and experiences are considered key to living satisfied lives and forging social relationships (Miller, 1994). This rings true for luxury also, and in African luxury brands the pleasures associated with luxury consumption are strongly linked to self-actualization and collective identity politics. Future African luxury research should further explore the extent to which pleasure and joy are encoded in luxury brands, products, and discourses, and the important roles that positive affect, expressed through material form, plays in the everyday lives of African consumers. This also relates to work in the sector: how can we better learn how luxury work takes place in African contexts, the forms of satisfaction and pleasure it might enable, for example in craftsmanship, and how is it similar or different to work in luxury sectors elsewhere in the world?

In terms of sustainability, this book has mostly considered the ways in which African luxury brands stake a claim for their economic and cultural importance. It has also highlighted how strong associations with nature are a key resource for producing a narrative of pride, and building an association with luxury. For future African luxury researchers, it will be important to track and explore what role luxury might play in future strategies for sustainability, both economic and environmental, within the consumer industries. How might African brands be positioned in such a way as to offer especially useful and progressive insights and strategies in that regard, considering the complexities of the commercial and regulatory environments in which they are already functioning and achieving success? Are "green" African luxury brands already in existence, and if not are they possible, and how might African creatives explore and take up new scientific innovations and ideas in their work?

The analysis presented in this short book has been, by necessity, limited. Nevertheless, I have offered a journey through some key visual material being produced by some important luxury creatives in South Africa. We have explored the heritage design work of Thebe Magugu, the magnificent bead necklaces of The Herd, and through these case studies learned about the innovative ways in which authenticity and culture are deployed through a moral claim of ownership. We have considered the feminist and Black pride politics that are embedded in brands selling products as simple as Gugu Intimates' underwear and Suki Suki's hair oil, and seen how minimalism and a connection to nature can be deployed to further the project of emancipation, to some degree at least. And we have considered the edgy queer aesthetics of urban streetwear as exemplified by Karabo Poppy's limited edition sneakers and Rich Mnisi's fetishistic luxury furniture design, in order to theorize new ways in which queer politics is interfacing with entrepreneurship on the continent. Huge opportunities exist for further critical luxury studies approaches to economic and cultural activity emanating on the continent of Africa. I hope to see many colleagues and postgraduate students in Africa and beyond exploring new case studies and new questions. This concluding chapter has attempted to map out some of the complexities of the bigger theoretical areas opened up by this close analysis on African luxury branding. I have already gestured at a few new questions and possible directions for research on African luxury branding. Future research might explore these, and other perspectives, on how African luxury brands and branding can continue to co-construct future worlds.

Appendix 1
Details on Interviews

Interview material is drawn on in minor, but important ways, in this book. As such, I wanted to offer some more detail on how interviews were used as a research method. This project received ethics committee approval through the University of the Witwatersrand Human Research Ethics Committee (Non-Medical).

I recruited participants initially through personal networks, and then through snowball sampling, and supplemented this with some cold-calling (with moderate success) when relevant opportunities arose. I intentionally kept my definitions of what qualified as a "luxury professional" quite open, so that through my conversations with people who were working in, or had worked in, any sector calling itself luxury, I would learn better how it was defined and deployed in multiple ways. I met and spoke with people working in a wide diversity of luxury sectors, from fashion to hospitality, from alcohol promotion to food, from jewellery to communications and transport. I spoke with men and women, from a range of ethnic backgrounds, located in cities around Africa (and indeed, beyond) who were formally employed by big companies, self-employed as consultants, or visionary entrepreneurs who had created impressive brands and operations from nothing. Although they were all different, and had different takes on the industry, and were facing unique opportunities and challenges in their home cities and national economies, all were united by the fact that they considered the idea of luxury to be central to their work, and indeed even their own professional identities. Each interview lasted from half an hour to an hour, and was recorded with permission. Where participants chose not to allow recording, detailed notes were taken before and after the discussion, with their permission. Recordings were transcribed by research assistants. Dozens of hours of recording and hundreds of pages of transcripts were generated. Interview transcripts were treated as an iteration of marketing discourse, and cited from in such a way as to develop an argument about the values, meanings, and ideas shaping African luxury branding more broadly.

Many of my interview participants have public profiles and are well-known in the industry, furthermore, many of them know one another either personally or by reputation. As such, even though my participants constituted experts who may often have been more than happy for their identities to be attached to their statements in my writings, the decision was taken to anonymize all reporting from the interviews. Each participant was given a pseudonym, and care was taken to ensure that they are not identifiable by reference to the names of their companies and brands, or any specifics to do with their work. Affording complete anonymity to research participants is crucial as it gives both participant and researcher greater freedom to speak their mind, and critically explore data, foregrounding the content of the discussions and the larger conceptual issues to which they are attached, respectively. When I quote from interviews in the rest of the book, I reference it by simply noting the pseudonym of the participant. It is worth noting, that as in any qualitative interview-based research project, some of my participants inevitably ended up being more central to how I have reported on the research in this book. This is because some of my participants had a naturally more expressive or articulate way of explaining the issues, which resonated perhaps a little more closely with the kind of issues that I wanted to study. Doubtless my own style of interviewing and holding the space affected this. As I reviewed transcripts, I noticed that in early interviews, I was more likely to muddle my questions, or ask them in a way that seemed to take certain ideas for granted, but as the process evolved and I spoke to more and more people, developing my own understanding and thinking in the process, I became better at asking open-ended questions that allowed me to get more insight into the ideas and opinions of my participants. As a qualitative methodology, interviews should be understood to be a process of exchange between interviewer and interviewee, which will evolve over time both in the context of each individual conversation's beginning and end, and the longitudinal matrix of all the interviews over the years in which they took place.

Finally, a word on when I knew that I had enough material. As luxury is a growing and dynamic sector on the continent, I was constantly identifying new potential interview participants. I followed up every lead that I could, and secured as many interviews as possible.

There did come a time, however, as I was accumulating perhaps the 35th interview, that I realized that I was starting to hear very similar ideas over and over again. I made note of that, and kept moving forward in order to ensure that I could cover ground that I hadn't yet covered, for example trying to make sure that I spoke to more people from west or east Africa, or from another luxury sector, such as jewellery. But by the time that I had arranged the 50th interview, I felt quite certain that I had exhausted – conceptually at least – what I could learn about luxury promotional culture in anglophone African cities for the purposes of my project. At this stage, I decided to stop, and turn my energies to analysis and writing.

Bibliography

Abad-Santos A and Grady C (2018) How Big Dick Energy explains modern masculinity. *Vox*, 27 June. Available at: https://www.vox.com/culture/2018/6/27/17506898/big-dick-energy-explained.

Abidin C (2016) "Aren't these just young, rich women doing vain things online?": Influencer selfies as subversive frivolity. *Social Media + Society* 2(2): 2056305116641342. DOI: 10.1177/2056305116641342.

Aliyev F and Wagner R (2018) Cultural influence on luxury value perceptions: Collectivist vs. individualist luxury perceptions. *Journal of International Consumer Marketing* 30(3): 158–172. DOI: 10.1080/08961530.2017.1381872.

Amankwah-Amoah J, Boso N and Debrah YA (2018) Africa rising in an emerging world: An international marketing perspective. *International Marketing Review* 35(4): 550–559. DOI: 10.1108/IMR-02-2017-0030.

Amatulli C and Guido G (2012) Externalised vs. internalised consumption of luxury goods: Propositions and implications for luxury retail marketing. *The International Review of Retail, Distribution and Consumer Research* 22(2): 189–207. DOI: 10.1080/09593969.2011.652647.

Ariztia T (2015) Unpacking insight: How consumers are qualified by advertising agencies. *Journal of Consumer Culture* 15(2): 143–162. DOI: 10.1177/1469540513493204.

Armitage J and Roberts J (eds) (2016a) *Critical Luxury Studies: Art, Design, Media*. Edinburgh: Edinburgh University Press.

Armitage J and Roberts J (2016b) The Spirit of Luxury. *Cultural Politics* 12(1): 1–22. DOI: 10.1215/17432197-3436283.

Aronczyk M and Powers D (2010) *Blowing Up the Brand: Critical Perspectives on Promotional Culture*. Peter Lang.

Arvidsson A (2005) *Brands: Meaning and Value in Media Culture*. Routledge.

Asongu SA and Odhiambo NM (2019) How enhancing information and communication technology has affected inequality in Africa for sustainable development: An empirical investigation. *Sustainable Development* 27(4): 647–656. DOI: 10.1002/sd.1929.

Atkinson R (2016) Limited exposure: Social concealment, mobility and engagement with public space by the super-rich in London. *Environment and Planning A* 48(7): 1302–1317. DOI: 10.1177/0308518X15598323.

Atwal G and Jain S (2012) *The Luxury Market in India: Maharajas to Masses.* Basingstoke: Palgrave Macmillan.

Azevedo MJ (2018) *Africana Studies: A Survey of Africa and the African Diaspora.* Carolina Academic Press.

Batat W (2019) *Digital Luxury: Transforming Brands and Consumer Experiences.* SAGE.

Beaverstock JV, Hubbard P and Rennie Short J (2004) Getting away with it? Exposing the geographies of the super-rich. *Geoforum* 35(4): 401–407. DOI: 10.1016/j.geoforum.2004.03.001.

Beavon K (2005) *Johannesburg: The Making and Shaping of the City.* Brill. Available at: https://brill.com/view/title/12542 (accessed 3 February 2020).

Becker D (2016) Instagram as a potential platform for alternative visual culture in South Africa. In: Bunce M, Franks S, and Paterson C (eds) *Africa's Media Image in the 21st Century: From the 'Heart of Darkness' to 'Africa Rising'.* London: Routledge.

Becker D (2019) Afrofuturism and decolonisation: Using Black Panther as methodology. *Image & Text* (33). DOI: 10.17159/2617-3255/2018/n33a7.

Berry CJ (1994) *The Idea of Luxury: A Conceptual and Historical Investigation.* Cambridge: Cambridge University Press.

Bhabha HK (2012) *The Location of Culture.* 2nd ed. Routledge. DOI: 10.4324/9780203820551.

Biyela NG (2013a) Colour metaphor in zulu culture: Courtship communication in beads. *American International Journal of Contemporary Research* 3(10): 37–41.

Biyela NG (2013b) The traditional 'Zulu Valentine'. *Indilinga African Journal of Indigenous Knowledge Systems* 13(1): 1–10.

Blake DA (2019) "It Ain't He, It Ain't She, It's We": The politics of self-definition and self-valuation in the androgynous model web series. *Dress* 45(1): 1–21. DOI: 10.1080/03612112.2019.1559529.

Bond P (2014) Africa Rising? Afro-optimism and uncivil society in an era of economic volatility. In: Obadare E (ed.) *The Handbook of Civil Society in Africa.* Nonprofit and Civil Society Studies. New York, NY: Springer New York, pp. 233–251. DOI: 10.1007/978-1-4614-8262-8_15.

Bosko D (1981) Why Basotho wear blankets. *African Studies* 40(1): 23–32. DOI: 10.1080/00020188108707567.

Bourdieu P (1984) *Distinction: A Social Critique of the Judgement of Taste.* Harvard University Press.

Brennan N and Gudelunas D (eds) (2017) *RuPaul's Drag Race and the Shifting Visibility of Drag Culture: The Boundaries of Reality TV.* 1st ed. 2017. Cham: Springer International Publishing: Imprint: Palgrave Macmillan. DOI: 10.1007/978-3-319-50618-0.

Bright J (2020) Africa e-tailer Jumia reports first full-year results post NYSE IPO. In: *TechCrunch.* Available at: https://social.techcrunch.com/2020/02/25/africa-e-tailer-jumia-reports-first-full-year-results-post-nyse-ipo/ (accessed 16 March 2021).

Brodin O, Coulibaly D and Ladwein R (2016) Subcultural ostensive luxury as a creative and mimetic process: The case of the Sapeurs Parisiens. *Recherche et Applications en Marketing (English Edition)*: 2051570715626373. DOI: 10.1177/2051570715626373.

Bunce M, Franks S and Paterson C (2016) *Africa's Media Image in the 21st Century: From the 'Heart of Darkness' to 'Africa Rising'*. Routledge.

Burke T (1996) *Lifebuoy Men, Lux Women: Commodification, Consumption, and Cleanliness in Modern Zimbabwe*. Durham: Duke University Press Books.

Byrd RP, Cole JB and Guy-Sheftall B (2009) *I Am Your Sister: Collected and Unpublished Writings of Audre Lorde*. Oxford University Press.

Caldeira SP (2020) "Shop it. Wear it. 'Gram it.": A qualitative textual analysis of women's glossy fashion magazines and their intertextual relationship with Instagram. *Feminist Media Studies* 20(1): 86–103. DOI: 10.1080/14680777. 2018.1548498.

Calefato P (2014) *Luxury: Fashion, Lifestyle and Excess*. A&C Black.

Camminga B (2019) *Transgender Refugees and the Imagined South Africa: Bodies Over Borders and Borders Over Bodies*. 1st ed. 2019. Global Queer Politics. Cham: Springer International Publishing: Imprint: Palgrave Macmillan. DOI: 10.1007/978-3-319-92669-8.

Campbell JE (2015) Gay and lesbian/queer markets/marketing. In: Cook DT and Ryan JM (eds) *The Wiley Blackwell Encyclopedia of Consumption and Consumer Studies*. Oxford, UK: John Wiley & Sons, Ltd, pp. 1–4. DOI: 10. 1002/9781118989463.wbeccs128.

Carolin A (2019) South African Gay Pages and the politics of whiteness. *Social Dynamics* 45(2): 234–249. DOI: 10.1080/02533952.2019.1619273.

Carrington A (2019) From blaxploitation to fan service: Watching Wakanda. *Safundi* 20(1): 5–8. DOI: 10.1080/17533171.2019.1552350.

Catanese BW (2010) Remembering Saartjie Baartman. *Atlantic Studies* 7(1): 47–62. DOI: 10.1080/14788810903515592.

Cavender R and Kincade DH (2014) Management of a luxury brand: Dimensions and sub-variables from a case study of LVMH. *Journal of Fashion Marketing and Management* 18(2): 231–248. DOI: 10.1108/JFMM-03-2013-0041.

Cham M (2009) Foreword. In: *Zulu Love Letter: A Screenplay*. Johannesburg: Wits University Press.

Chatterjee D (2020) Cultural appropriation: Yours, mine, theirs or a new intercultural? *Studies in Costume & Performance* 5(1): 53–71. DOI: 10.1386/scp_00013_1.

Cheng AA (2011a) *Second Skin: Josephine Baker & the Modern Surface*. Oxford: Oxford University Press, USA.

Cheng AA (2011b) Shine: On Race, Glamour, and the Modern. *PMLA* 126(4): 1022–1041. DOI: 10.1632/pmla.2011.126.4.1022.

Chevalier M and Lu PX (2011) *Luxury China: Market Opportunities and Potential*. John Wiley & Sons.

Chevalier M and Mazzalovo G (2012) *Luxury Brand Management: A World of Privilege*. John Wiley & Sons.

Choi JW (Jimmy) and Kim M (2019) Sneakerhead brand community netno-graphy: An exploratory research. *Fashion, Style & Popular Culture* 6(2): 141–158. DOI: 10.1386/fspc.6.2.141_1.

Chouliaraki L (2008) The media as moral education: Mediation and action. *Media, culture & society* 30(6): 831–852.

Coetzee C (2019) Between the world and Wakanda. *Safundi* 20(1): 22–25. DOI: 10.1080/17533171.2019.1551739.

Cohan M (2021) Illustrator Karabo Poppy's take on sneaker culture celebrates African design. *CNN Style*, 22 February. African Voices. Atlanta. Available at: https://edition.cnn.com/style/article/karabo-poppy-south-africa-illustrator-nike-sneakers-spc-intl/index.html.

Coleman R (2020) *Glitterworlds: The Future Politics of a Ubiquitous Thing.* London: Goldsmiths Press. Available at: https://books.google.co.za/books?id=KFzUyQEACAAJ&dq=Glitterworlds:+The+Future+Politics+of+a+Ubiquitous+Thing&hl=en&sa=X&ved=2ahUKEwiJ1oW7pqXuAhVcwuYKHYMnC8QQ6AEwAHoECAAQAg (accessed 18 January 2021).

Collins PH (2000) *Black Feminist Thought: Knowledge, Consciousness and the Politics of Empowerment.* New York: Routledge.

Comaroff J and Comaroff JL (2012) Theory from the South: Or, how Euro-America is Evolving Toward Africa. *Anthropological Forum* 22(2): 113–131. DOI: 10.1080/00664677.2012.694169.

Cowart K and Wagner P (2021) An investigation of androgyny and sexual orientation in advertising: How androgynous imagery and sexual orienta-tion impact advertisement and brand attitudes. *Journal of Advertising Research*: JAR-2021-001. DOI: 10.2501/JAR-2021-001.

Cramer C, Sender J and Oqubay A (2020) *African Economic Development: Evidence, Theory, Policy.* 1st ed. Oxford University Press. DOI: 10.1093/oso/9780198832331.001.0001.

Crenshaw K, Gotanda N, Peller G, et al. (1995) *Critical Race Theory: The Key Writings That Formed the Movement.* The New Press.

Cronin AM (2004) Regimes of mediation: advertising practitioners as cultural intermediaries? *Consumption Markets & Culture* 7(4): 349–369. DOI: 10.1080/1025386042000316315.

Cui AP, Wajda TA and Walsh MF (2015) Luxury brands in emerging markets: A case study on China. In: *Entrepreneurship in International Marketing.* Advances in International Marketing 25. Emerald Group Publishing Limited, pp. 287–305. Available at: http://www.emeraldinsight.com/doi/abs/10.1108/S1474-797920140000025013 (accessed 10 February 2015).

Dabiri E (2016) Why I am (still) not an Afropolitan. *Journal of African Cultural Studies* 28(1): 104–108. DOI: 10.1080/13696815.2015.1100066.

Dale SK, Pierre-Louis C, Bogart LM, et al. (2018) Still I rise: The need for self-validation and self-care in the midst of adversities faced by Black women with HIV. *Cultural Diversity and Ethnic Minority Psychology* 24(1): 15–25. DOI: 10.1037/cdp0000165.

David OO and Grobler W (2020) Information and communication technology penetration level as an impetus for economic growth and development in Africa. *Economic Research-Ekonomska Istraživanja* 33(1): 1394–1418. DOI: 10.1080/1331677X.2020.1745661.

De Beukelaer C (2017) Toward an 'African' take on the cultural and creative industries? *Media, Culture & Society* 39(4): 582–591. DOI: 10.1177/0163443 716664856.

De Bortoli L (2018) CK One: A shared fragrance. Corporeità e sessualità gender-free. *Ocula* 19. DOI: 10.12977/ocula2018-1.

Declue J (2016) Let's play: Exploring cinematic black lesbian fantasy, pleasure and pain. In: Johnson EP (ed.) *No Tea, No Shade: New Writings in Black Queer Studies*. Durham: Duke University Press, pp. 216–238.

Dei GJS and Lordan M (2016) *Anti-Colonial Theory and Decolonial Praxis*. Peter Lang Publishing, Incorporated.

Diniz C (2014) *The Luxury Market in Brazil: Market Opportunities and Potential*. Springer.

Disemelo K (2015) *Black Men as Pink Consumers?: A Critical Reading of Race, Sexuality and the Construction of the Pink Economy in South African Queer Consumer Media*. Masters Dissertation. University of the Witwatersrand, Johannesburg.

Disemelo K (2019a) Decolonising visual culture: Critical Perspectives and Approaches. In: Chiumbu S and Iqani M (eds) *Media Studies: Critical African and Decolonial Approaches*. Cape Town: Oxford University Press, pp. 261–277. Available at: https://www.oxford.co.za/book/9780190443535-media-studies-critical-african-and-decolonial-approaches#.YCKEdnczbwc (accessed 9 February 2021).

Disemelo K (2019b) Performing the queer archive: Strategies of self-styling on instagram. In: Pather J and Boulle C (eds) *Acts of Transgression Contemporary Live Art in South Africa*. Johannesburg: Wits University Press: Wits University Press, pp. 219–242. Available at: http://search.ebscohost.com/login.aspx?direct=true&scope=site&db=nlebk&AN=1899003 (accessed 12 August 2021).

Disemelo K (2021) *The House of Indigo: An Ethnographic Study of Drag Performance, Beauty Pageantry, and Cosmopolitan Femininity in Johannesburg*. PhD Dissertation. University of the Witwatersrand, Johannesburg.

Dorling D (2015) *Inequality and the 1%*. London: Verso.

Dosekun S (2019) The playful and privileged Africanicity of Luxury @AlaraLagos. In: Iqani M and Dosekun S (eds) *African Luxury: Aesthetics and Politics*. Bristol: Intellect Books, pp. 93–106.

Dosekun S (2020) *Fashioning Postfeminism: Spectacular Femininity and Transnational Culture*. Champaign: University of Illinois Press.

Duggan L (2020) The new homonormativity: The Sexual politics of neoliberalism. In: Castronovo R, Nelson DD, and Pease DE (eds) *Materializing Democracy*. Duke University Press, pp. 175–194. DOI: 10.1515/9780822383901-008.

Elias AS, Gill R and Scharff C (2017) *Aesthetic Labour: Rethinking Beauty Politics in Neoliberalism*. Springer.

Erfurt-Cooper P (2009) The health and wellness concept: A global overview. In: Cooper M and Erfurt-Cooper P (eds) *Health and Wellness Tourism*. Berlin: De Gruyter, pp. 25–48. DOI: 10.21832/9781845411138-004.

Factora J (2021) Three LGBTQ+ people have been killed in South Africa during pride month. *Them.*, 15 June. Available at: https://www.them.us/story/three-lgbtq-people-killed-south-africa-during-pride-month.

Falkof N (2022) Consuming Africa: Safari aesthetics in the johannesburg beauty industry. *Consumption Markets & Culture* 25(1).

Farber L (2010) Africanising hybridity? Toward an Afropolitan aesthetic in contemporary South African fashion design. *Critical Arts* 24(1): 128–167. DOI: 10.1080/02560040903509234.

Fasselt R (2015) "I'm not Afropolitan — I'm of the Continent": A conversation with Yewande Omotoso. *The Journal of Commonwealth Literature* 50(2): 231–246. DOI: 10.1177/0021989414552922.

Featherstone M (2014) Luxury, consumer culture and sumptuary dynamics. *Luxury* 1(1): 47–69. DOI: 10.2752/205118174X14066464962436.

Featherstone M (2016) LuxusA thanatology of luxury from nero to bataille. *Cultural Politics* 12(1): 66–82. DOI: 10.1215/17432197-3436391.

Feldman J (2017) Stella mccartney accused of cultural appropriation for using ankara prints in her spring collection. *Huff Post*, 5 October. Available at: https://www.huffpost.com/entry/stella-mccartney-cultural-appropriation_n_59d62f70e4b0becae802b7d0.

Ferguson J (2006) *Global Shadows: Africa in the Neoliberal World Order*. Duke University Press.

Forrest R, Koh SY and Wissink B (2017) *Cities and the Super-Rich: Real Estate, Elite Practices and Urban Political Economies*. Springer.

Foster LA (2017) *Reinventing Hoodia: Peoples, Plants, and Patents in South Africa. Feminist technosciences*. Seattle: University of Washington Press.

Francis D, Valodia I and Webster E (2020) *Inequality Studies from the Global South*. Routledge.

Frans RPE and Aryani MI (2020) The influences of fashion as a soft power towards france's economic growth. *WIMAYA* 1(02): 31–39. DOI: 10.33005/wimaya.v1i02.35.

Freberg K, Graham K, McGaughey K, et al. (2011) Who are the social media influencers? A study of public perceptions of personality. *Public Relations Review* 37(1): 90–92. DOI: 10.1016/j.pubrev.2010.11.001.

Frosh P (2015) Selfies| the gestural image: The selfie, photography theory, and kinesthetic sociability. *International Journal of Communication* 9(0): 1607–1628.

Gagliardone I (2016) *The Politics of Technology in Africa*. Cambridge University Press.

Ganahl JP (2014) *Corruption, Good Governance, and the African State: A Critical Analysis of the Political-Economic Foundations of Corruption in Sub-Saharan Africa*. Universitätsverlag Potsdam.

Geczy A and Karaminas V (2020) *Queer Style*. Available at: https://doi.org/
10.5040/9781350050723?locatt=label:secondary_bloomsburyCollections
(accessed 17 August 2021).

Gill R (2007) Postfeminist media culture Elements of a sensibility. *European
Journal of Cultural Studies* 10(2): 147–166. DOI: 10.1177/13675494
07075898.

Godart F (2014) The power structure of the fashion industry: Fashion capitals,
globalization and creativity. *International Journal of Fashion Studies* 1(1):
39–55. DOI: 10.1386/infs.1.1.39_1.

Golding P and Harris P (1996) *Beyond Cultural Imperialism: Globalization,
Communication and the New International Order*. SAGE.

Gondola ChD (1999) Dream and drama: The search for elegance among
congolese youth. *African Studies Review* 42(01): 23–48. DOI: 10.2307/
525527.

Gqola P (2001) Ufanele uqavile: Blackwomen, feminisms and postcoloniality
in Africa. *Agenda* 16(50): 11–22. DOI: 10.1080/10130950.2001.9675990.

Gqola PD (2010) *What Is Slavery to Me? Postcolonial/Slave Memory in Post-
Apartheid South Africa*. Johannesburg: Wits University Press.

Halberstam J (2018) *Female Masculinity*. Twentieth anniversary edition with a
new preface. Durham: Duke University Press.

Hall S (2020) The west and the rest: Discourse and power [1992]. In: *Essential
Essays, Volume 2*. Duke University Press, pp. 141–184. DOI: 10.1515/97814
78002710-010.

Hammersley M and Atkinson P (1995) Writing ethnography. In: *Ethnography:
Principles in Practice*. London: Routledge, pp. 239–262.

Hardy J (2010) *Cross-Media Promotion*. Peter Lang.

Hardy J (2014) *Critical Political Economy of the Media: An Introduction*.
Communication and society. London: Routledge.

Haseler S (2000) *The Super-Rich: The Unjust New World of Global Capitalism*.
Basingstoke: Palgrave Macmillan.

Havnevik K (2015) The current Afro-optimism – A realistic image of Africa?
FLEKS - Scandinavian Journal of Intercultural Theory and Practice 2(2).
DOI: 10.7577/fleks.1498.

Hay I (2013) *Geographies of the Super-Rich*. Cheltenham: Edward Elgar
Publishing.

Hay I and Beaverstock JV (2016) *Handbook on Wealth and the Super-Rich*.
Cheltenham: Edward Elgar Publishing.

Hay I and Muller S (2012) 'That tiny, stratospheric apex that owns most of the
world' – Exploring geographies of the super-rich. *Geographical Research*
50(1): 75–88. DOI: 10.1111/j.1745-5871.2011.00739.x.

Healy MJ, Beverland MB, Oppewal H, et al. (2007) Understanding retail
experiences - the case for ethnography. *International Journal of Market
Research* 49(6): 751–778. DOI: 10.1177/147078530704900608.

Heine K (2010) The personality of luxury fashion brands. *Journal of Global
Fashion Marketing* 1(3): 154–163. DOI: 10.1080/20932685.2010.10593067.

Hesmondhalgh D (2007) *The Cultural Industries*. SAGE.

Hilderbrand L (2013) "Luring Disco Dollies to a Life of Vice": Queer Pop Music's Moment: Luring Disco Dollies to a Life of Vice. *Journal of Popular Music Studies* 25(4): 415–438. DOI: 10.1111/jpms.12044.

Hofmeyr I (2014) Against the global south. In: *WITS-Michigan Workshops*, Johannesburg, 2014. WISER, University of Johannesburg.

Holt DB (2002) Why do brands cause trouble? A dialectical theory of consumer culture and branding. *Journal of Consumer Research* 29(1): 70–90. DOI: 10.1086/jcr.2002.29.issue-1.

Holt DB (2004) *How Brands Become Icons: The Principles of Cultural Branding*. Harvard Business Press.

Hooks bell (2007) *Ain't I a Woman: Black Women and Feminism*. Cambridge, Massachusetts: South End Press.

Hooks bell (2014) *Talking Back: Thinking Feminist, Thinking Black*. Taylor & Francis.

Howell S and Vincent L (2014) 'Licking the snake' – The i'khothane and contemporary township youth identities in South Africa. *South African Review of Sociology* 45(2): 60–77.

Hudders L and Pandelaere M (2011) The silver lining of materialism: The impact of luxury consumption on subjective well-being. *Journal of Happiness Studies* 13(3): 411–437. DOI: 10.1007/s10902-011-9271-9.

Hunter M (2007) The persistent problem of colorism: Skin tone, status, and inequality. *Sociology Compass* 1(1): 237–254. DOI: 10.1111/j.1751-9020. 2007.00006.x.

Hunter M (2011) Shake it, Baby, Shake it: Consumption and the New Gender Relation in Hip-Hop. *Sociological Perspectives* 54(1): 15–36. DOI: 10.1525/ sop.2011.54.1.15.

Hunter M (2013) The consequences of colorism. In: Hall RE (ed.) *The Melanin Millennium*. Amsterdam: Springer Netherlands, pp. 247–256. Available at: http://link.springer.com/chapter/10.1007/978-94-007-4608-4_16 (accessed 10 November 2014).

Hunter ML (2002) "If you're light you're alright" light skin color as social capital for women of color. *Gender & Society* 16(2): 175–193. DOI: 10.1177/ 08912430222104895.

Iqani M (2012a) *Consumer Culture and the Media: Magazines in the Public Eye*. London: Palgrave Macmillan.

Iqani M (2012b) Smooth bodywork: The role of texture in images of cars and women on consumer magazine covers. *Social Semiotics* 22(3): 311–331. DOI: 10.1080/10350330.2012.665261.

Iqani M (2015) Agency and affordability: Being black and 'middle class' in South Africa in 1989. *Critical Arts* 29(2): 126–145. DOI: 10.1080/02560046.2 015.1039200.

Iqani M (2016) *Consumption, Media and the Global South: Aspiration Contested*. London: Palgrave Macmillan.

Iqani M (2018) Performing post-feminist wealth: The intersectional aesthetics of irene major's instagram profile. *Australian Feminist Studies* 33(96): 209–222. DOI: 10.1080/08164649.2018.1517246.

Iqani M (2019) The last luxury frontier? How global consulting firms discursively construct the African market. In: Iqani M and Dosekun S (eds) *African Luxury: Aesthetics and Politics*. Bristol: Intellect Books.

Iqani M (2020) Luxury as a new humanitarianism? Ethical discourses in African creative entrepreneurship. In: Chouliaraki L and Vestergaard A (eds) *Routledge Handbook of Humanitarian Communication*. London: Routledge.

Iqani M (2021) The influencer interface: Local social media marketing of global luxury brands in African cities. *Journal of Design, Business & Society* 7(1): 105–121.

Iqani M (2022) Glitter, Shine, Glow: Patinas of feminine achievement in south african celebrity portraiture. *Cultural Politics* 18(1).

Iqani M (In Press) The crooked codes of the luxury handbag: Narratives of empowered feminine consumption in Africa. *Feminist Economics*.

Iqani M and Dosekun S (eds) (2019) *African Luxury: Aesthetics and Politics*. Bristol: Intellect Books.

Iqani M and Kenny B (2017) *Consumption, Media and Culture in South Africa: Perspectives on Freedom and the Public*. Routledge.

Iqani M and Schroeder JE (2016) #Selfie: Digital self-portraits as commodity form and consumption practice. *Consumption Markets & Culture* 19(5): 405–415. DOI: 10.1080/10253866.2015.1116784.

Irvin G (2008) *Super Rich: The Rise of Inequality in Britain and the United States*. Cambridge: Polity.

Jackson PA (2009) Capitalism and global queering: National markets, parallels among sexual cultures, and multiple queer modernities. *GLQ: A Journal of Lesbian and Gay Studies* 15(3): 357–395. DOI: 10.1215/10642684-2008-029.

James D (2014) *Money from Nothing: Indebtedness and Aspiration in South Africa*. Stanford University Press.

Jaworski A and Thurlow C (2017) Mediatizing the "super-rich," normalizing privilege. *Social Semiotics* 27(3): 276–287. DOI: 10.1080/10350330.2017.1301792.

Jedlowski A (2012) Small screen cinema: Informality and remediation in nollywood. *Television & New Media*: 1527476412443089. DOI: 10.1177/1527476412443089.

Jedlowski A (2017) African media and the corporate takeover: Video film circulation in the age of neoliberal transformations. *African Affairs* 116(465): 671–691. DOI: 10.1093/afraf/adx017.

Jewitt C (2009) *The Routledge Handbook of Multimodal Analysis*. Routledge Chapman & Hall.

Jin B and Cedrola E (2017) *Fashion Branding and Communication: Core Strategies of European Luxury Brands*. Springer.

Jones A, DeFilippis JN and Yarbrough MW (eds) (2018) *The Unfinished Queer Agenda after Marriage Equality*. 1 Edition. London: Routledge, Taylor & Francis Group.

Kates SM (1999) Making the Ad perfectly queer: Marketing "Normality" to the Gay Men's Community? *Journal of Advertising* 28(1): 25–37. DOI: 10. 1080/00913367.1999.10673574.

Kates SM and Belk RW (2001) The meanings of lesbian and gay pride day: Resistance through consumption and resistance to consumption. *Journal of Contemporary Ethnography* 30(4): 392–429. DOI: 10.1177/089124101030004003.

Kedzior R and Allen DE (2016) From liberation to control: Understanding the selfie experience. *European Journal of Marketing*. DOI: 10.1108/EJM-07-2015-0512.

Khamis S, Ang L and Welling R (2017) Self-branding, 'micro-celebrity' and the rise of Social Media Influencers. *Celebrity Studies* 8(2): 191–208. DOI: 10.1080/19392397.2016.1218292.

Klein K (2020) Band-Aid launches bandages to 'embrace the beauty of diverse skin'. *Dezeen*, June. Available at: https://www.dezeen.com/2020/06/16/band-aid-bandages-brown-black-skin-tones/.

Krause-Wahl A, Löffler P and Söll Ä (eds) (2021) *Materials, Practices and Politics of Shine in Modern Art and Popular Culture*. Material culture of art and design. London; New York: Bloomsbury Visual Arts.

Kress G (2013) *Multimodality: A Social Semiotic Approach to Contemporary Communication*. Routledge.

Kress G and Leeuwen T van (2001) *Multimodal Discourse*. London: Bloomsbury Academic.

Kuldova T (2016) *Luxury Indian Fashion: A Social Critique*. Bloomsbury Publishing.

Kuntsman A (2017) *Selfie Citizenship*. Springer.

Kupe T (2013) Globalization from my African corner. *Media, Culture & Society* 35(1): 139–146. DOI: 10.1177/0163443712464568.

Labase S (2017) 'I want to make women feel beautiful in their own skin' – Gugu Intimates founder. *True Love*, 29 March. Available at: https://www.news24.com/truelove/Archive/i-want-to-make-women-feel-beautiful-in-their-own-skin-gugu-intimates-founder-20170728.

Laden S (2003) Who's Afraid of a Black Bourgeoisie? Consumer Magazines for Black South Africans as an Apparatus of Change. *Journal of Consumer Culture* 3(2): 191–216. DOI: 10.1177/14695405030032003.

Larraufie A-FM and Kourdoughli A (2014) The e-semiotics of luxury. *Journal of Global Fashion Marketing* 5(3): 197–208. DOI: 10.1080/20932685.2014.906120.

Lazarsfeld PF (1941) Remarks on administrative and critical communications research. *Studies in Philosophy and Social Science* 9(1): 2–16.

Leaver T, Highfield T and Abidin C (2020) *Instagram: Visual Social Media Cultures*. John Wiley & Sons.

Lenard PT and Balint P (2020) What is (the wrong of) cultural appropriation? *Ethnicities* 20(2): 331–352. DOI: 10.1177/1468796819866498.

Levander C and Mignolo W (2011) Introduction: The global south and world Dis/Order. *The Global South* 5(1): 1–11. DOI: 10.2979/globalsouth.5.1.1.

Levin N (2015) I am Saartjie Baartman. In: Mistry J, Schuhmann A, and Ruckteschell K (eds) *Gaze Regimes: Film and Feminisms in Africa.* Johannesburg: Wits University Press.

Ligaga D (2014) Mapping emerging constructions of good time girls in Kenyan popular media. *Journal of African Cultural Studies* 26(3): 249–261.

Ligaga D (2016) Presence, agency and popularity: Kenyan "Socialites", Femininities and digital media. *Eastern African Literary and Cultural Studies* 2(3–4): 111–123. DOI: 10.1080/23277408.2016.1272184.

Liu ZJ, Yildirim P and Zhang ZJ (2018) *A Theory of Minimalist Luxury.* ID 3246729, SSRN Scholarly Paper, 16 September. Rochester, NY: Social Science Research Network. DOI: 10.2139/ssrn.3246729.

Loureiro SMC and Kaufmann HR (2016) Luxury values as drivers for affective commitment: The case of luxury car tribes. *Cogent Business & Management* Wright LT (ed.) 3(1): 1171192. DOI: 10.1080/23311975.2016.1171192.

Lunde KS (2019) Ancient, indigenous and iconic textile motifs in contemporary fashion. *Textile Society of America Symposium Proceedings.* DOI: 10.32873/unl.dc.tsasp.0039.

Lux M and Bug P (2018) Sole value – The sneaker resale market: An explorative analysis of the sneaker resale market. Hochschule Reutlingen. Available at: https://publikationen.reutlingen-university.de/frontdoor/index/index/docId/2118 (accessed 17 March 2021).

Magubane Z (2004) *Bringing the Empire Home: Race, Class, and Gender in Britain and Colonial South Africa.* Chicago: University of Chicago Press.

Mahajan V (2011) *Africa Rising: How 900 Million African Consumers Offer More Than You Think.* New Jersey: Pearson Prentice Hall.

Maingard J (2009) Love, loss, memory and truth. In: *Zulu Love Letter: A Screenplay.* Johannesburg: Wits University Press.

Marwick AE (2015) Instafame: Luxury selfies in the attention economy. *Public Culture* 27(1 75): 137–160. DOI: 10.1215/08992363-2798379.

Mason H (2017) #Gauteng52, Week 19: Where basotho blankets are made. In: *2Summers.* Available at: https://2summers.net/2017/05/09/gauteng52-week-19-basotho-blankets-made/.

Matebeni Z (2018) Ihlazo: Pride and the politics of race and space in Johannesburg and Cape Town. *Critical African Studies* 10(3): 315–328. DOI: 10.1080/21681392.2019.1610008.

Matebeni Z, Monro S and Reddy V (eds) (2018) *Queer in Africa: LGBTQI Identities, Citizenship, and Activism.* 1st ed. Routledge. DOI: 10.4324/9781315406749.

Matthews D, Cryer-Coupet Q and Degirmencioglu N (2021) I wear, therefore I am: Investigating sneakerhead culture, social identity, and brand preference among men. *Fashion and Textiles* 8(1): 1. DOI: 10.1186/s40691-020-00228-3.

Mazzarella W (2003) *Shoveling Smoke: Advertising and Globalization in Contemporary India.* Durham: Duke University Press.

Mbilishaka A (2018) PsychoHairapy: Using Hair as an entry point into black women's spiritual and mental health. *Meridians: Feminism, Race, Transnationalism* 16(2): 382–392.

McEwen H (2019) Suspect sexualities: Contextualizing rumours of homosexuality within colonial histories of population control. *Critical African Studies* 11(3): 266–284. DOI: 10.1080/21681392.2019.1670701.

McNeil P and Riello G (2016) *Luxury: A Rich History.* Oxford University Press.

Mignolo WD and Walsh CE (2018) *On Decoloniality: Concepts, Analytics, Praxis.* Duke University Press.

Miller D (1994) *Material Culture and Mass Consumption.* Blackwell.

Miller D (1997) *Capitalism: An Ethnographic Approach.* Berg.

Miller D (1998) *A Theory of Shopping.* Polity Press.

Miller D (2001) *Consumption: Theory and Issues in the Study of Consumption.* Taylor & Francis.

Miller D (2013) *Consumption and Its Consequences.* John Wiley & Sons.

Miranda-Vilela AL, Botelho AJ and Muehlmann LA (2014) An overview of chemical straightening of human hair: Technical aspects, potential risks to hair fibre and health and legal issues. *International Journal of Cosmetic Science* 36(1): 2–11. DOI: 10.1111/ics.12093.

Mokoena H (2019) African Utopianism: The Invention of Africa in Diesel's The Daily African – A Retrogressive Reading. In: Iqani M and Dosekun S (eds) *African Luxury: Aesthetics and Politics.* Bristol: Intellect Books, pp. 37–56.

Montez R (2020) *Keith Haring's Line: Race and the Performance of Desire.* Durham: Duke University Press.

Morhart F and Malär L (2020) Authenticity in luxury branding. In: Morhart F, Wilcox K, and Czellar S (eds) *Research Handbook on Luxury Branding.* Edward Elgar Publishing, pp. 190–207. DOI: 10.4337/9781786436351. 00023.

Moser R and Narayanamurthy G (2016) Middle East luxury retail sector – Opportunities or uncertainties in the future? *Emerald Emerging Markets Case Studies* 6(3): 1–39. DOI: 10.1108/EEMCS-05-2014-0146.

Mosher CM, Levitt HM and Manley E (2006) Layers of leather: The identity formation of leathermen as a process of transforming meanings of masculinity. *Journal of Homosexuality* 51(3): 93–123. DOI: 10.1300/J082v51 n03_06.

Muholi Z (2018) *Zanele Muholi: Somnyama Ngonyama, Hail the Dark Lioness.* New York, NY: Aperture.

Muholi Z (2020) *Zanele Muholi.* Allen S and Nakamori Y (eds). London: Tate Publishing.

Murray S (2002) Africaine: Candice breitz wangechi mutu tracey rose fatimah tuggar. *Nka: Journal of Contemporary African Art* 16: 88–93.

Musila GA (2015) *A Death Retold in Truth and Rumour: Kenya, Britain and the Julie Ward Murder*. Boydell & Brewer.

Ndemo B and Weiss T (2016) *Digital Kenya: An Entrepreneurial Revolution in the Making*. Springer.

Ndlovu T (2022) Managing sullied pleasure: dining out while black and middle class in South Africa. *Consumption Markets & Culture* 25(4): 382–394. DOI: 10.1080/10253866.2021.1987227.

Nettleton A (2009) Beadwork and visual praise poems. In: *Zulu Love Letter: A Screenplay*. Johannesburg: Wits University Press.

Nettleton ACE (ed.) (2015) *Beadwork, Art and the Body: Dilo Tše Dintshi = Abundance*. South Africa: Wits Art Museum: Wits University Press.

Newell S (2012) *The Modernity Bluff: Crime, Consumption, and Citizenship in Côte D'Ivoire*. University of Chicago Press.

Nickel PM (2016) Luxury linesordering and the formation of regard and disregard. *Cultural Politics* 12(1): 54–65. DOI: 10.1215/17432197-3436367.

Nixon S (2003) *Advertising Cultures: Gender, Commerce, Creativity*. London: SAGE.

Nixon R (2013) *Slow Violence and the Environmentalism of the Poor*. Harvard University Press.

Norwood CR (2018) Decolonizing my hair, unshackling my curls: An auto-ethnography on what makes my natural hair journey a Black feminist statement. *International Feminist Journal of Politics* 20(1): 69–84. DOI: 10.1080/14616742.2017.1369890.

Nye JS (1990) Soft power. *Foreign Policy* (80). *Washingtonpost*. Newsweek Interactive, LLC: 153–171. DOI: 10.2307/1148580.

Nye JS (2009) Get smart: Combining hard and soft power. *Foreign Affairs* 88(4): 160–163.

Nyong'o T (2012) Queer Africa and the fantasy of virtual participation. *Women's Studies Quarterly* 40(1–2): 40–63.

Nyong'o T (2018) *Afro-Fabulations: The Queer Drama of Black Life*. NYU Press.

Ochoa JD (2015) Shine bright like a migrant: Julio salgado's digital art and its use of 'Jotería'. *Social Justice* 42(3/4 (142)). Social Justice/Global Options: 184–199.

Okonkwo U (2010) *Luxury Online: Styles, Systems, Strategies*. Springer.

Okonkwo U (2016) *Luxury Fashion Branding: Trends, Tactics, Techniques*. Springer.

Onwudiwe E and Ibelema M (eds) (2003) *Afro-Optimism: Perspectives on Africa's Advances*. Westport, Conn: Praeger.

Oyekunle OA (2017) The contribution of creative industries to sustainable urban development in South Africa. *African Journal of Science, Technology, Innovation and Development* 9(5): 607–616. DOI: 10.1080/20421338.2017.1327932.

Pellot B (ed.) (2021) *Hopes and Dreams That Sound Like Yours: Stories of Queer Activism in Sub-Saharan Africa*. Johannesburg: MaThoko's Books. Available at: https://gala.co.za/books-and-resources/publications-and-publishing/mathokos-books/hopes-and-dreams/.

Peterson B (2009) Writer's Statement: Trauma, Art and Healing. In: *Zulu Love Letter: A Screenplay*. Johannesburg: Wits University Press.

Peterson B (2021) A love letter to those who passed on and those still tasked with creating a better future for all. *Safundi* 22(1): 23–25. DOI: 10.1080/17533171.2020.1823741.

Pheto-Moeti B (2020) *The meaning and symbolism of cultural dress practices in Lesotho*. PhD Dissertation. University of the Free State, Bloemfontein.

Pilane P and Iqani M (2016) Miss-represented: A critical analysis of the visibility of black women in South African Glamour magazine. *Communicare: Journal for Communication Sciences in Southern Africa* 35(1): 126–171.

Pinto S (2013) *Difficult Diasporas: The Transnational Feminist Aesthetic of the Black Atlantic*. NYU Press.

Posel D (2010) Races to consume: revisiting South Africa's history of race, consumption and the struggle for freedom. *Ethnic and Racial Studies* 33(2): 157–175. DOI: 10.1080/01419870903428505.

Posel D and Van Wyk I (eds) (2019) *Conspicuous Consumption in Africa*. Johannesburg: Wits University Press.

Potts J and Cunningham S (2008) Four models of the creative industries. *International Journal of Cultural Policy* 14(3): 233–247. DOI: 10.1080/10286630802281780.

Pratt ML (2008) *Imperial Eyes: Travel Writing and Transculturation*. Second edition. London New York: Routledge.

Prestholdt J (2007) *Domesticating the World: African Consumerism and the Genealogies of Globalization*. University of California Press.

Ramadan Z and Nsouli NZ (2021) Luxury fashion start-up brands' digital strategies with female Gen Y in the Middle East. *Journal of Fashion Marketing and Management: An International Journal* (ahead-of-print). DOI: 10.1108/JFMM-10-2020-0222.

Roach C (1997) Cultural imperialism and resistance in media theory and literary theory. *Media, Culture & Society* 19(1): 47–66. DOI: 10.1177/016344397019001004.

Roach CM (2002) *Mother/Nature: Popular Culture and Environmental Ethics*. Bloomington, IN: Indiana University Press.

Roberts J (2019) Is contemporary luxury morally acceptable? A question for the super-rich. *Cultural Politics* 15(1): 48–63. DOI: 10.1215/17432197-7289486.

Rocamora A (2016) Online luxury: Geographies of production and consumption and the louis vuitton website. In: Armitage J and Roberts J (eds) *Critical Luxury Studies: Art, Design, Media*. Edinburgh: Edinburgh University Press, pp. 199–220.

Rosenberg L, Turunen LLM, Järvelä S-M, et al. (2020) The handbag. *Consumption Markets & Culture* 0(0): 1–8. DOI: 10.1080/10253866.2020.1756269.

Rovai S (2016) *Luxury the Chinese Way: The Emergence of a New Competitive Scenario*. Springer.

Schiller HI (1976) *Communication and Cultural Domination.* White Plains, NY: Sharpe.

Schroeder J, Borgerson J and Wu Z (2017) A brand culture approach to chinese cultural heritage brands. In: Balmer JMT and Chen W (eds) *Advances in Chinese Brand Management.* London: Palgrave Macmillan UK, pp. 80–106. DOI: 10.1057/978-1-352-00011-5_4.

Schroeder JE (2002) *Visual Consumption.* London: Routledge.

Schroeder JE (2007) Critical visual analysis. In: Belk RW (ed.) *Handbook of Qualitative Research Methods in Marketing.* London: Edward Elgar Publishing, pp. 303–321.

Schroeder JE (2008) *Visual Analysis of Images in Brand Culture.* ID 941431, SSRN Scholarly Paper. Rochester, NY: Social Science Research Network. Available at: http://papers.ssrn.com/abstract=941431 (accessed 3 January 2015).

Schroeder JE and Borgerson J (2012) Dark desires: Fetishism, ontology and representation in contemporary advertising. In: Reichert T and Lambiase J (eds) *Sex in Advertising: Perspectives on the Erotic Appeal.* New York: Routledge, pp. 65–89. Available at: https://www.taylorfrancis.com/books/e/9781410607065 (accessed 17 August 2021).

Scotch RK (2009) 'Nothing About Us Without Us': Disability Rights in America. *OAH Magazine of History* 23(3): 17–22. DOI: 10.1093/maghis/23.3.17.

Scott KD (2017) *The Language of Strong Black Womanhood: Myths, Models, Messages, and a New Mandate for Self-Care.* Lanham: Lexington Books.

Sender K (1999) Selling sexual subjectivities: Audiences respond to gay window advertising. *Critical Studies in Mass Communication* 16(2): 172–196. DOI: 10.1080/15295039909367085.

Septianto F, Seo Y, Sung B, et al. (2020) Authenticity and exclusivity appeals in luxury advertising: The role of promotion and prevention pride. *European Journal of Marketing* 54(6): 1305–1323. DOI: 10.1108/EJM-10-2018-0690.

Serafini P and Maguire JS (2019) Questioning the super-richrepresentations, Structures, Experiences. *Cultural Politics* 15(1): 1–14. DOI: 10.1215/174321 97-7289444.

Seringhaus FHR (2005) Selling luxury brands online. *Journal of Internet Commerce* 4(1): 1–25. DOI: 10.1300/J179v04n01_01.

Sherry JF, Kozinets RV, Storm D, et al. (2001) Being in the zone staging retail theater at espn zone chicago. *Journal of Contemporary Ethnography* 30(4): 465–510. DOI: 10.1177/089124101030004005.

Shetty V, Shetty N and Nair D (2013) Chemical hair relaxers have adverse effects a myth or reality. *International Journal of Trichology* 5(1): 26. DOI: 10.4103/0974-7753.114710.

Sidiropoulos E (2014) South africa's emerging soft power. *Current History* 113(763): 197–202. DOI: 10.1525/curh.2014.113.763.197.

Smith N (2015) Queer in/and sexual economies. In: Laing MW, Pilcher K, and Smith N (eds) *Queer Sex Work.* Routledge studies in crime and society 14. London; New York: Routledge, Taylor & Francis Group.

Sobande F (2019) Woke-washing: "Intersectional" femvertising and branding "woke" bravery. *European Journal of Marketing* 54(11): 2723–2745. DOI: 10.1108/EJM-02-2019-0134.

Sobopha MP (2001) Returning the gaze: Cape Town one city festival. *Nka: Journal of Contemporary African Art* 13(1): 56–61.

Soldow G (2013) Homoeroticism in advertising: Something for everyone with androgyny. In: Reichert T and Lambiase J (eds) *Sex in Consumer Culture The Erotic Content of Media and Marketing*. Available at: http://www.vlebooks.com/vleweb/product/openreader?id=none&isbn=9780203810729 (accessed 17 August 2021).

Spronk R (2012) *Ambiguous Pleasures: Sexuality and Middle Class Self-Perceptions in Nairobi*. Berghahn Books.

Staszak J-F (2015) Performing race and gender: The exoticization of josephine baker and anna may wong. *Gender, Place & Culture* 22(5): 626–643. DOI: 10.1080/0966369X.2014.885885.

Tamale S (2020) *Decolonization and Afro-Feminism*. Daraja Press.

Taylor I (2014) Is Africa Rising Rise of Africa. *Brown Journal of World Affairs* 21: 143–162.

Thomas LM (2012) Race, bodies and beauty skin lighteners, black consumers and jewish entrepreneurs in South Africa. *History Workshop Journal*: dbr017. DOI: 10.1093/hwj/dbr017.

Thomas LM (2020) *Beneath the Surface: A Transnational History of Skin Lighteners*. Duke University Press.

Thompson KA (2015) *Shine: The Visual Economy of Light in African Diasporic Aesthetic Practice*. Duke University Press.

Thrift N (2008) The material practices of glamour. *Journal of Cultural Economy* 1(1): 9–23.

Thussu D (2016) *Communicating India's Soft Power: Buddha to Bollywood*. Place of publication not identified: Palgrave Macmillan.

Thussu DK and Nordenstreng K (eds) (2015) *Mapping BRICS Media*. London: Routledge. Available at: http://www.sponpress.com/books/details/9781138026254/ (accessed 25 February 2015).

Tigner AL (2008) The flowers of paradise: Botanical trade in sixteenth- and seventeenth-century england. In: Sebek B and Deng S (eds) *Global Traffic*. New York: Palgrave Macmillan US, pp. 137–156. DOI: 10.1057/978023 0611818_8.

Tomlinson J (2012) Cultural imperialism. In: *The Wiley-Blackwell Encyclopedia of Globalization*. John Wiley & Sons, Ltd. Available at: http://onlinelibrary.wiley.com/doi/10.1002/9780470670590.wbeog129/abstract (accessed 8 February 2015).

Treviño AJ, Harris MA and Wallace D (2008) What's so critical about critical race theory? *Contemporary Justice Review* 11(1): 7–10. DOI: 10.1080/102825 80701850330.

Truong Y, Simmons G, McColl R, et al. (2008) Status and conspicuousness –
Are they related? Strategic marketing implications for luxury brands.
Journal of Strategic Marketing 16(3): 189–203. DOI: 10.1080/0965254
0802117124.

Twitchell JB (2013) *Living It up: Our Love Affair with Luxury.* New York:
Columbia University Press.

Vänskä A (2014) From gay to queer—Or, wasn't fashion always already a very
queer thing? *Fashion Theory* 18(4): 447–463. DOI: 10.2752/175174114X13
996533400079.

Veblen T (2007) *The Theory of the Leisure Class.* Oxford University Press.

Vigneron F and Johnson LW (2004) Measuring perceptions of brand luxury.
The Journal of Brand Management 11(6): 484–506. DOI: 10.1057/
palgrave.bm.2540194.

Walker C, Bohlin A, Hall R, et al. (2010) *Land, Memory, Reconstruction, and
Justice: Perspectives on Land Claims in South Africa.* Ohio University Press.

Walley K, Custance P, Copley P, et al. (2013) The key dimensions of luxury
from a UK consumers' perspective. *Marketing Intelligence & Planning* 31(7):
823–837. DOI: 10.1108/MIP-09-2012-0092.

Wang Y and Song Y (2013) Counterfeiting: Friend or foe of luxury brands?
An examination of chinese consumers' attitudes toward counterfeit luxury
brands. *Journal of Global Marketing* 26(4): 173–187. DOI: 10.1080/08911
762.2013.804618.

Williamson S (2002) Thembinkosi Goniwe: ArtBio. *Art Throb*, October.
Available at: https://artthrob.co.za/02oct/artbio.html.

Xulu C (2002) *Colour Coding and its Meaning in Zulu Women's Beadwork: A
Study of Zulu Women's Beadwork in Fashion Design and Decoration.*
Masters Dissertation. University of KwaZulu-Natal, Durban.

Yusoff K (2018) *A Billion Black Anthropocenes or None.* Minneapolis: U of
Minnesota Press.

Zhiyan W, Schroeder J and Borgerson J (2013) *From Chinese Brand Culture to
Global Brands: Insights from Aesthetics, Fashion and History.* Houndmills,
Basingstoke, Hampshire, UK; New York, NY: Palgrave Macmillan.

Index

9781032129617